# Pilgrimage

## Reflections of
## a Medjugorje Priest

# Pilgrimage

## Reflections of
## a Medjugorje Priest

Svetozar Kraljevic, OFM

While the apparitions of Medjugorje have yet to be formally approved by the Church, on their tenth anniversary in June of 1991, four bishops of the Vatican Commission led the evening Eucharistic service, while more than a hundred priests heard confessions. As at Lourdes, while each person must draw his or her own conclusion about the witness of the visionaries, the Sacraments and the preaching of the Gospel remain the central events in Medjugorje.

# Table of Contents

# Foreword

*The Apparitions of Our Lady of Medjugorje* by Father Svetozar Kraljevic, was the first I had read on the mystical events which had begun some seven summers before in the village with the unpronounceable name. There, in the central mountains of what was still known as Yugoslavia, the Blessed Virgin Mary had appeared to six young people, much as she previously had at Fatima and Lourdes. In Medjugorje, however, she was still appearing to four of the six, every afternoon at the same time.

Fifteen million pilgrims had come from all over the world to be part of what was happening here, and now I, too, was present, collaborating on a book project with Wayne Weible which had already filled several hours of interview tapes. Glancing at my notepad where I'd outlined some questions to put to this diminutive priest, I switched on the micro-recorder and brought my eyes up to his ... and forgot everything.

But in that moment, my own pilgrimage took on a new depth and meaning. There were many more interviews scheduled—and little opportunity to spend time with this man. But there was enough for God to say: *Here is a surrendered life; learn from it.*

When I returned to Medjugorje five months later, still working on the collaboration, there was more time. Fr. Svet invited me up to Konjic, to have supper at his monastery, with four other friars and two sisters, none of whom spoke English. Nonetheless, I felt a part of their meal, even of the humorous banter which I did not understand. The contentment and fulfillment of their shared life needed no translation.

When I first broached the possibility of his doing a book about his own childhood and vocation, followed by reflections, Fr. Svet was loathe to consider it. He was convinced that there was nothing in his life that would be of interest to anyone. He had an abhorrence of being singled out in any way: "Part of the calling of a Franciscan is not only to physical poverty, but to poverty of mind and spirit," he explained. "It is not appropriate for a Franciscan to be remembered. It is for the work of the Church to be remembered. If a priest is assigned to a parish or a monastery, he merely assumes the work of those who have gone before—and will come after. His name will be quickly forgotten—as it should be."

I pointed out that it was not his life which would be presented, but rather what God had done in such a life. God, not he, would receive the credit, which was as it should be.

A year passed before I again raised the subject, this time during one of his visits to the States. He had written pieces in English on pornography and abortion, and he did admit that he would welcome the oppor-

tunity to speak out on such things, as well as on behalf
of vocations and the necessity for prayer. In a book he
could warn people of the world view that was tearing
apart the family. And he could explore the meaning of
pilgrimage—not only to Medjugorje, but the journey
which came after it, and which lasted the rest of one's
life.

After another year, he agreed. I interviewed him
in New York, on Cape Cod, in Konjic, and finally at
a Franciscan retreat house. Like many Croatians, he
was part poet, and it frustrated him that he did not
have the fluency in English that he had in his native
tongue.

Yet with the instinctive humility, there was also
much humor. He could be pensive, filled with sorrow
or compassion, or far wiser than one might expect of
his 39 years. But mostly there was joy. He loved to
tease, yet it was the gentlest teasing I had ever known.
Indeed, I never heard him say an ungentle thing about
anyone. No wonder, then, that at the mere mention of
his name, a spontaneous smile comes to the lips of all
who know him.

The final work on this book was completed in
July of 1991, at the Provincial retreat house in the
tiny hamlet of Glavaticevo, so high in the mountains
above Konjic that the Neretva River was no more than
a fast-running stream. Here, sheep grazed the moun-
tainsides, and the red-tiled roofs were steeply sloped
to shed snow, as in the Alps. From the hilltop of the
retreat house, the eye delighted in picking a path between the small, well-kept fields, up higher past the
last flock, to the distant hazy summit of one of the en-
circling mountains. The view was breathtaking—and

so picturesque that it belonged on a box of expensive Swiss chocolates.

Also at the house were eight young men from the province, on a week's retreat prior to becoming friar-novices. The retreat was led by the Vice Provincial of Franciscans, Fr. Tomislav Pervan (whom I had interviewed when he was pastor of St James). Boisterous when they arrived, the young men soon quieted and bonded together, on the eve of the most important transition in their lives. At the same time, their individual personalities began to emerge, and when I asked Fr. Svet if he could tell which in twenty years would be strong priests and which would have difficulties, he simply nodded. Then he said, "But do not count out God; something might happen in a heart that would change everything."

On the last day, he took the eight young men and me up a mountain path to visit the homes of four different families. For each we carried a kilo of coffee beans which for them would be a luxury, not a staple. It was a perfect day for climbing—clear and sunny but not humid, with just enough breeze. Our path took us gently upward, occasionally crossing a cold, tumbling stream or opening unexpectedly onto a spectacular vista which would startle us with how far we had ascended.

At the first house, set half into the side of the mountain, we were greeted by an old woman with two teeth left in her smile. Her face was seamed with age, and she leaned on a stick, as she invited us into the front room of her two-room abode. There, she insisted on serving us refreshments, though she could not have had two dinars to rub together.

She doted on Fr. Svet as if he were her son, and the way he listened to whatever it was she was so earnestly telling him, it was as if there was nothing more important to him, no other demands on his time.

This was more than a pastor's heart, I thought; this was what Jesus would have done. When we left, it was Fr. Svet who was in awe. "Do you know," he confided to me, "it takes her three hours to walk down to church." He shook his head. "And she does it every Sunday."

We climbed higher. I tried to remember if I had ever been to a year-round residence back home which was not accessible by car; I could not think of one. Finally we reached the homes of two families who lived close together, three generations farming the land and now also cutting wood to sell, for there was no work to be had in the valley. Here we would stop for lunch, which we had brought with us, bread and cheese and sausage—enough for all.

But they would not be outgiven, producing pieces of chicken, cucumbers and onions, apricots and little cakes. These people, too, were delighted to have us; in fact, it was like a party. I glanced over at Fr. Svet; he was radiant. At first I attributed his happiness to his leaving the pressures of the world far below—and the constant tension of being in that world but not of it. But then I remembered that he had been born and raised in the mountains, with people like these. He was home.

That evening, our last in Glavaticevo, Fr. Tomislav and Fr. Svet went out after supper to one of the cars and bent over the radio to hear the news about the war in Croatia, which was certain to spill over into Bosnia and Hercegovina very soon.

It seemed that it would take a miracle to save Croatia now—and neighboring Hercegovina—from a bloodbath. The hatred between Serbs and Croats ran as deep as that between Catholics and Protestants in Northern Ireland, or between Jews and Palestinians in the Holy Land. Present for so long that it was now ingrained in the racial memories of these two peoples, it had been suppressed under Communist rule. But now the Communists were no longer in power.

The next morning, Fr. Svet took me for a walk in the little graveyard on the hill behind the retreat house. Pointing out two large unmarked graves, he told me that after the war the *partizani* had come here and killed thirty villagers, after first making them dig these graves. He knew that if there was war, there would be fresh graves. And there would be priests in them.

Yet he had the faith to believe for the miracle of peace. He asked me what message I thought Medjugorje (and this book) might have for the leaders on both sides who would be responsible for whatever was coming.

"Accountability!" I exclaimed. "Most of them have forgotten—if they ever knew—that they will have to stand before God and answer to Him for every life that He had entrusted into their care, for every drop of blood needlessly shed."

He thought about that for a moment, then said: "The message for the leaders, for the politicians, is the Truth. If they will see the Truth and come to know it, they will do it. And the Truth will set them, and everyone else, free."

Fr. Svet always gave the benefit of the doubt, even to politicians. That could be frustrating—until one recalled that Jesus had done the same thing (often to the consternation of his followers). Once a person embraced the Truth, His Truth, whatever he had previously done—or been—was irrelevant.

PanAm, which at the outbreak of hostilities had ceased operations into Yugoslavia, was sending a plane on Sunday to Zagreb and Dubrovnik, to pick up stragglers. As I drove down to the coast with a disc-copy of the corrected manuscript in my pocket (and another tucked away in my shaving kit), I could not help but wonder if I would ever see my friend again.

Perhaps common sense *would* prevail. It never had before in the Balkans—but then, Mary had never appeared there before. Perhaps enough people would respond to her appeal to pray with the heart for peace....

— David Manuel
Editor

# 1

# Mountains

On a hazy, summer afternoon, the distant mountains seem almost inviting. Not gray and hard and formidable, as at other times. And at dusk, when their peaks are fired by the setting sun, their splendor stuns. Visitors see them that way.

But the people who live in them don't. For the mountains are within them.

The mountains of Hercegovina, in the center of the country still known to many as Yugoslavia, were the first reality of my childhood. My parents and our neighbors farmed their slopes and dwelt in their hollows. And when they had to go somewhere, they did not go around; they went over. It would never occur to them to do otherwise, and they expected their children to do the same.

From my earliest recollection, the mountains were a central feature in our lives. They did not give much of a living, but we did not need much. They taught us to be satisfied with what we had. In a way, they

1

were like parents; they shaped our lives. And our outlook on life. The Croatians of Hercegovina, those who
have lived for generations hundreds of meters above
the sea, have taken on the characteristics of the mountains. Calm, steady, quiet, they endure....

The other reality was God. Like the mountains He
was just there—in my parents' prayers, in their plans,
in their Sunday worship at the little church an hour's
walk away. And so He was there for me, too. In the
hills next to our house, in the trees, in the cows, in the
two cats who were my only playmates, God was an
ever-present reality....

Where we lived there were three houses, built by
my father and his two brothers. They were typical
mountain dwellings—one room with a dirt floor mea-
suring perhaps four by four meters. I was the young-
est child there by several years; in fact, by the logic of
today I should not have been born. My father was 46
and my mother 41; they had already had six children,
four of whom were alive, and in the mountains after
the war there was total deprivation. The Nazis and the
*partizani* had left no crops, no livestock, nothing. All
the people had was trust in God.

It is hard to imagine circumstances less favorable
into which to bring an infant, yet terminating an un-
wanted pregnancy was unthinkable. Each life, no matter how inconvenient or unfortunate its environment,
was given by God. For His purpose and as His blessing, though the blessing was not always readily ap-
parent. Two of my four surviving brothers and sisters
(two others had died as small children) were Mongol-
oids. My parents loved them, and so we loved them,
too. God gave them to us, but it was not always easy

to care for them. Not until they died years later did we realize what special people they were.

Some might regard such a circumstance as a suffering or a punishment. But the one who dares to live with suffering through to its completion will discover that it is actually a great gift. Some people are difficult to live with, difficult to love. Sometimes the old or the new or the genetically defective can be a trial. But instead of routinely putting them in nursing homes or institutions—or killing them before they can be born—what if we were to live with them? What if, when our love is exhausted, we were to ask God to give us *His* love for them? Eventually we will discover the blessing they can be. And who knows, perhaps in the process we will become more what He intended us to be—which may have been part of His purpose.

In our village of Podvranic in the parish of Kocerin, about thirty kilometers northwest of the city of Mostar, there was no school. So at seven my mother walked me over the mountains to the school in Rujan, a village two kilometers away. The school was one room with benches like pews, and my mother told the teacher the name of her son and left. Quickly I sat on the first bench that had some room on it. "Not there, not next to the girls!" the teacher shook her finger at me. "You go over there and sit with the boys!" I went and did not remember another thing.

They gave me a used book and bag, and I walked home with them, the way my mother and I had come. The next morning, when it was time to leave for school, I stood by the door with my book bag. My mother said, "What are you waiting for?"

"I'm waiting to go to school."

"Then why don't you go?"

"I'm waiting for you."

"You go alone today, Sveto."

And so I took my first step into the world alone—bare-footed, as did many of the mountain children. When you have nothing, parents cannot buy you shoes. My older brother's old shoes would not fit me for several years. One morning a few months later, where the path to school crossed a road, a truck came by and slowed to offer me a lift. I was delighted to get a ride and come to school much earlier! The driver stopped at the path leading to the school. There was a little store there, and to my surprise the truck driver motioned to me to come inside with him. In the store, he talked to the clerk who pointed to a shelf full of popular rubber shoes. They had cloth linings, very cheap, but they were magnificent!

The clerk tried several on me, until one pair fit. I could not believe what was happening. Then, as the truck driver paid him, a neighbor who had been watching all of this said, "God will reward you for that."

Undoubtedly He has; they were the finest. God and this little child will never forget.

# 2

# Peace

The first awareness of every pilgrim coming to Medjugorje is the presence of the mountains. If they are driving from Dubrovnik, before long the mountains begin to rise from beside the road and loom above them. If they are following the Neretva River down from Sarajevo, they are in the river gorge, surrounded by mountains. If they are flying into Mostar or coming by train, it is the same—mountains, mountains, mountains.

The first awareness of any child was learning to walk in the mountains—barefooted, over rocky ground, and always climbing or descending. People walked in them to visit friends, go to church, to school, or simply to look after the sheep. They were a part of me—just as they are a part of everyone who lives there. You can see it in their faces.

For me, they are very gentle, very beautiful—like the palm of God's hand, holding you. But only as long as you are reconciled with them. You have to reconcile yourself to the fact that often your destination will be inaccessible by car—even if you have one. You are going to have to walk, to climb.

The mountain is telling you that you cannot control it, you cannot remove it, you cannot even wish that it was not there. Because it is there—so powerfully. And each time you climb it, it will touch you, make your heart beat harder, make you sweat. Make you allow extra time to get where you are going.

But if you can accept that, and be reconciled with the mountain, you will have peace.

A mountain is an intimate place. If you live with a mountain, then you come to know its caves, its particular rocks, the way it breathes, the way it lives. It is like knowing God.

As a child, I would like to play God. I would climb to the top of a steep mountain, find a big rock which was not tight in the ground, and push it off of there. It would roll down, crashing, knocking loose other rocks, making a great noise in its wild dance. It would have a sense of power—of strength, speed and destruction. But in the end, it would be tamed. It would come to rest, at peace, never to move again. Sometimes our lives are like that.

There was one particularly steep mountain near us that as a child I came to know well. We had seven lambs, and it was my duty to take them there. I also came to know the lambs well. Their leader was Cula, and she was always in front. If there was ever anyone to cause trouble, it was her. She would lead the rest of them into every place they weren't supposed to go. I was seven and very upset with her—until we became friends. After that, it was easy. Because once you have the leader, you have the rest of the gang.

Sometimes, there would be extra bread that my mother made for lunch, and I would give it to them. After that, as soon as they saw me, they would run up to me. I could go anywhere, and they would follow me. But there was a problem: when it was time for lunch, they would want mine. I wasn't sure I wanted to share it with them. It was too far to go home, so I would climb a tree and eat it there with the seven little lambs around the base of the tree looking up at me.

Once in a while, there was a *real* problem: one of the lambs would get lost. Then a search would have to be made to find it, because you could not go home without it. But these sheep were my friends, my companions in those early years, and I have loved animals ever since.

In the mountains we see the power of God, which goes so much further than anything man is capable of. It is a creative power; He put these rock formations together in an incredibly beautiful way. All who see them are awed. Those who know Him, are inspired.

For the pilgrim, the mountains symbolize both the hardship of life and the beauty of God's creation. This is a land which will not feed you, which will not even feed your lambs. This is a land you come to see and experience and respect, and then return to where you live.

For those of us who live here, the mountains have another role. Man comes into this world basically selfish. The mountains break that selfishness. They teach him patience and humility. They will not give him what he demands, but they will give him what he needs. And they will teach him to be content with that.

Few people in my parish in Konjic have cars. For some, there are not even roads to their homes. They climb the mountains every day, sometimes twice a day. They climb when it is hot, and when it is cold, when it is raining or snowing. They do it their whole lives. The gardens outside their houses are small; there is not much soil and no room to make them any larger. So they will remain that size for when their children are teaching their children to grow vegetables there.

The mountains teach reality. If it takes an hour to walk to church, then you do not start a task that will take an hour, when you have less than an hour before you must leave. You do not fantasize that this time, it will take you only 45 minutes to walk to church. The mountains have taught you better than that. They have taught you that you begin your preparation for the Mass when you begin the last chore that you do before leaving the house. The mountains have taught the people of Konjic well; they are always on time.

You live in the mountains, and you grow to love them—to see the majesty of God's design, from the white fire of a snow-capped peak in the noon sun right down to a lone thistle nestled behind a protecting rock.

The rain, the cold of winter, the fatigue are always there, always challenging—but you are reconciled with the mountains, and you are at peace.

# 3

# The Faith

The world I grew up in was less sophisticated than today. There were fewer options, and that meant fewer temptations. My parents did things a certain way, because that was the way their parents had done them, and their parents' parents. When you are born into that, you accept it; everyone did—it would never occur to them to do otherwise.

My world was the parish of Kocerin in the mountains of Hercegovina. In it, three things loomed large—so large we normally would not think to mention them, because they were a part of us. There were the mountains—and God—and the two were sometimes one. The other thing was the faith.

For countless generations, our people were born into the reality of the faith. God and the Sacrament and the Church were not questioned. In spiritual matters, the main guidance came from the priest. It always had.

With the leadership of the Church lay the main road, and having been born into that, you trusted it.

In Hercegovina it had always been that way. When the Croatian people first came to this land in the 7th and 8th centuries, Roman Catholic missionaries came to them. This was the easternmost outpost of the Church of Rome.

The Franciscan order was formally established in this region at the end of the 13th century, when St. Nicolas Tavelic came to preach against the powerful anti-Christian sect known as the Bogumils. Then, at the beginning of the 16th century, the Turks invaded from the east. While Shakespeare was writing his sonnets, the Croatian people were absorbing the brunt of the Turkish onslaught. They were subdued, but they were also a wall, protecting Western civilization by containing the advance of Islam.

The monasteries and churches of the mountain parish of Konjic where I am now assigned were completely destroyed. The buildings were burned down, the priests slain. A few escaped into the mountains, where they managed to keep the faith alive. They would hold secret Masses in the wilderness, and administer the other Sacraments. If they were discovered, all would be killed.

Every year, my mother used to go to pay homage at Ricina, the site of such a massacre. She would sit me on a rock nearby, while on her knees she would crawl around that place in prayer. Years later I would see in that act, the history of the faith of our people.

The Ottoman Turks realized that to extinguish the flame of Christianity, they must find and liquidate all of the priests. A great many were martyred, but they were unable to liquidate the faith.

The priests became legends—ghosts in brown robes who would be there when you needed them. And who would vanish when the clandestine Mass—or marriage service or funeral—was ended. The people never forgot what their priests did for them during the three hundred years of Turkish oppression. They told their children and grand children how the priests had constantly risked torture and execution to keep the faith alive. And they told me. When I was growing up, the brown-robed ones were heroes.

Eventually the Austro-Hungarian Empire prevailed over the Ottoman Empire, and in the late 19th century, Roman Catholicism was again welcome in Hercegovina. All, however, was not peaceful. There had always been difficulties between the Croats and the neighboring Orthodox Serbs, which periodically erupted into violence. On both sides were wounds going back many generations—wounds which were never allowed to heal.

Sometimes men prefer to hate. They feed on it, nurture their young on it, and derive a steely pleasure out of contemplating revenge. It is a poison which drips like acid into the reservoir of their souls, corroding their hearts from within. There is an antidote; it is manifesting itself now, in their very midst. *Pray for peace... repent... forgive...* soft words, gently spoken. But those who hate do not want to hear them; they prefer the taste of ashes. To sight along the blade and test its edge with their thumb.

The next chapter in the history of our faith can be found in the Provincial Headquarters of the Franciscan Order in Hercegovina, in the city of Mostar. Here, in a cupboard in a small room is a book bound in black leather. It is a large book, the size of a ledger, and it is very old; the leather is crumbling, and the book must be handled with great care. This is *The Book of the Dead*, the record of when and where and how each Franciscan priest and friar in the province has died.

With the end of the war and the coming of the Communists, the entries greatly increased. Few priests in those days died of natural causes. They were machine-gunned, or executed in the town square, or bound and thrown into the Neretva River. They served in their churches as long as they could, knowing that at any moment they might be confronted by the conquerors. When that time came, there could be no compromise, no backing down. If that was the point at which God required them to give their lives for the faith, then so be it.

This was the history of the faith that we grew up with, and why the brown-robed ones had a special place in the hearts of my parents and the people of Hercegovina. The Communists actually had very little effect on the faith there, though they were committed to smothering it, if they could. The trust in the church was rooted centuries deep and was stronger than any persecution. It ran like a vein of granite through the mountains.

And so the Government was set against the people. To get ahead, you had to have the Government's approval, and that meant renouncing your faith, and living without God. Very few were willing to do that. For most, life became a matter of survival, with much suffering and deprivation. Seldom did anyone speak of it. My Father said little against the Communists and their system, but he would never accept anything from them and would never do things their way.

The faith remained strong.

A surprising number of Government officials were Communists by day but Christians by night. There is the story of the guardian of a monastery going to the president of his county and demanding, "You should pay my electricity bill!"

"What do you mean?"

"You should pay my bill, because I use all that electricity at night, having hidden marriages for your officials, your police, your teachers."

Sometimes officials who were known to be sympathetic to the faith, had to act against it. An official of the school, for instance, would come for the Sacrament of marriage at night, and then a few months later would punish the children who went for their religious classes. He had no choice in the matter; he had to carry out the wishes of his superiors. But it must have caused him great inner anguish.

Through all the darkness and oppression, the light of the faith remained a beacon. It was not just a part of my childhood; it was part of me.

# 4

# Vocation

In Hercegovina, when a boy has completed eight years of school, he must decide what profession he will pursue. That is a difficult decision at any time, but for a boy of fifteen it is enormous. So—I prepared for it by playing soccer with my friends all day. On the next day we would go down to the trade school and apply to become auto mechanics.

But in the morning the others went alone. I did not join the others. When I had returned after the soccer game in the evening and told my brother what I was about to do, he was surprised. "I always thought you were going to be a priest," he said. And then I was the one who was surprised. For that was the one encouragement my heart needed. He had dropped a seed into prepared soil.

Occasionally the thought had come that I might be a priest. My earliest recollection of a particular priest was when I was five. My uncle had taken me to Mass with him, and when it was over, and we were about to walk home over the mountain, an immense rain came.

Those who were still there hurried for the shelter of the rectory, where we crowded into the little hallway there, waiting for the rain to stop. The priest came, and as he made his way through, he noticed this little boy, cold and wet, squeezed by all the big people packed into that space. He asked the housekeeper to bring me some bread and a bit of smoked meat. How good it tasted! His name was Fr. Milivoj Bebek, and (I learned later) he had just been released from eight years in prison.

This was another act of kindness that the little child would never forget. It meant so much to me—more than any much larger act would mean now. I saw later that in that act, I experienced a recognition of God's love. In the words of Jesus, "Whatsoever you do for these little ones, you do for me."

Well, there were many excellent professions, many worthy callings. But in my family the one which received the greatest respect was the priesthood. It was always spoken of as *the* vocation.

And now there was another factor: it was something opposing Communism. The Communists were seen as an extremely negative force in society and in the world. The priesthood was God's response, absolutely vital to the survival of society.

Weighing against such a decision was my scholastic record. The academic training for the priesthood was rigorous and demanding, which was a real concern. I may have had the head for it, but not the attitude. I seldom did homework, preferring soccer to studies. As a result, my second language, German, was terrible—and facility in language was given much emphasis in seminary. On the whole, considering my academic record, it would be a miracle to be accepted into the seminary program.

Nonetheless, the following morning, instead of accompanying my friends to the trade school, I took my scholastic documents to the rectory and presented them to the pastor. Two weeks later, he informed me that I had been accepted and would start my seminary training in the fall, in the city of Split.

The seminary high-school was a totally new experience for me. Always before, I had slept in a room with my entire family, always sharing the bed. Now suddenly I had a bed for myself, and twenty boys from all over Croatia as roommates. I spent much of that first night staring at the ceiling in the dark. And when I did fall asleep, I dreamed of the mountains and even of Cula and her gang of lambs.

But in the morning we were too busy preparing for the future, to dwell long in the past. The school was on the site of what was the great Franciscan seminary high-school, church, and monastery, *Poljud, Split.* My companions and I were being prepared for the priesthood in what was surely the best of all possible worlds. Now there would be no more fights or bad feelings, no more hurts or hurtful people. The perfect world was to begin—or so I thought.

I was soon brought back to earth. We had brought few personal belongings with us, and really needed no more than the half a drawer assigned to each of us. At that time it was the fashion for boys of that age to carry pocket knives. Mine was small but nice, with a good-quality blade. It was the one thing of value I owned, and in two days it was missing from my drawer.

I realized then, that this new world, though different, had its own difficulties, challenges—and wounds. Future priests faced the same temptations as anyone else. Years later, I would see that it was precisely this—the human fallibility of the priesthood—which enabled servants of God to lead others to Him. When they were living up to their vocation, priests were living proof that it *was* possible for ordinary men to put God first in all matters.

Jesus led by His example. Tempted in all things, He always made the right choice. A priest—and any man or woman—is always graced to make the right choice. It may be a hard choice, but there is grace sufficient. And if they make the right choice often enough, long enough, true holiness will eventually follow. And others will be inspired to go and do likewise.

St Francis once exhorted his followers: "Evangelize, evangelize! And if you must, use words."


The first year of seminary high-school was extremely difficult. I had never learned how to study, how to discipline the mind. Or the heart. The heart had to learn that science came before soccer, history before fiction, calculus before conversation. The heart rebelled, and every so often it would simply do what it wanted to do, not what it should do. (It still does.)

But becoming a priest was more important than becoming skilled at soccer, and I managed to work hard enough to stay in school. And then, in my fourth year, something happened: the school became something to enjoy. I don't know what caused the change; perhaps it was an intriguing course—or simply growing up. But to my surprise school and studying became a source of self-discovery and fulfillment. My scholastic average improved—not outstanding but very good, and it remained so throughout my academic career.

Looking back, it was more the sheer grace of God than anything else. I was in my vocation, doing what He intended me to do, and struggling to do my best. God honors obedience.

Something else happened in that fourth year. My sister came to visit me. She was on her way to Austria, where she could earn a better living, and she was nervous traveling alone on the train. She asked if I could accompany her as far as Zagreb. My superiors agreed, and soon we were underway. It was my first trip to a major city, and the first time I had missed a class in four years. It was an exciting adventure, and on my way home I was relaxed and happy. Sitting opposite me on the return train was an old man in his 70's. When he learned that I was a student at seminary, he told me that he had been with the *partizani,* when they had liberated *Siroki Brijeg.*

Before the war, *Siroki Brijeg* ("wide hill") was famous as a place of learning, with fine laboratories and facilities, a learned faculty, a museum with a collection of precious and semi-precious stones, and an extensive library. The friars, he said, had fired on them.

When I couldn't believe it, he insisted that it was true. He had seen them with his own eyes—friars in their habits, shooting rifles at him and his comrades from the windows and towers of the monastery.

I was speechless. He had to be wrong! And yet— why would he lie?

The moment I reached the seminary, I went to find Father Jakov Bubalo, a professor of history and a good friend whose counsel I had come to trust. I poured out the story to him, and he hesitated before replying. (In those days the Secret Police were everywhere; even to speak of such things was to risk imprisonment.) Then he decided to confide in me.

Siroki Brijeg was, of course, independent of any political affiliation, a mission working for the people and the Kingdom of God. But it was seen by the Communists as a great stronghold of the Church and a national, cultural center. They knew how deep ran the bonds between the people and the Franciscans—so deep that they dared not close the churches for fear of a popular uprising.

Now, as the tide of battle swept towards Siroki Brijeg, and the Communists gained control of the region, they saw a rare opportunity to discredit the Church. Ahead of the main body of the partizani, they sent trusted agents to the monastery, where they rounded up the twelve friars, the faculty of the school who were still there. They killed them and threw their bodies into an unused bomb shelter. Then donning the dead friars' robes and positioning themselves at upper windows where they could be easily seen, they fired at the first *partizani* to arrive, before throwing off the robes and fleeing.

With that pretext, the Communists could now destroy Siroki Brijeg. They brought all the books of the library and the classrooms into one place, as well as the rock collection, the laboratory equipment, everything. They poured gasoline on them, and set them afire, and then to the fire they added all the records of the parish—of births, baptisms, marriages, funerals, some going back for centuries. The church itself was demolished, and the other buildings were turned over to the Government.

The story the old partisan had told me had been repeated many times. Most people simply refused to believe friars could do such a thing. And yet, concluded Fr. Bubalo, there would always be some who wanted to believe it, and others who would ask themselves: why should anyone make up such a thing?

These were things I weighed, as I approached the priesthood. To become a priest was not going to be walking forth onto prepared ground. If you were fortunate, you would go where a holy priest had gone before you. Then the people would love the sight of your robe and would welcome you with open hearts. (Such an assignment, of course, would have its own difficulties, for they would also expect much of you.)

On the other hand, if your predecessor had not always made the right choices, then you would have hard ground to break and much nurturing of the soil.

Either way, in the end you were going to have to plow your own field, with no one to guide you but God.

Your mission would be to carry on a work which had begun long before you were born and would continue long after your death. While you wore the robe, you would, like a bridge, do your utmost in the best tradition of the friars who had established the mission, always creative, as they were.

# 5

# Legacy of Fear

During this time of preparation, I also began to realize on a deeper level just how much the struggle between Communism and the Church was a spiritual one. It was a contest for the hearts—and eternal souls—of the people. Those in religious vocations—and any true followers of Christ—were called to a life of sacrificial obedience and anonymous servanthood. The Communist Party, to *its* faithful, promised the opposite.

Initially it flattered the intellect, appealing to idealists who put their faith in man. They saw man not as a fallen creature, saved by grace, but as inherently good. Man did not need a Saviour, a Redeemer; collectively he had all the necessary skills and mind and abilities to provide for his needs. And given the opportunity, he would care for his neighbor. The Brotherhood of Man did not need the Fatherhood of God. The secular society, through the institutions of the State, would do the work of the Church.

At first glance, the Communist system did seem fairer than the old oppressive monarchies with their rigid class structure, or the weak and failed democracies of Christendom. *From each according to his abilities, to each according to his need*—what could be fairer than that? Christianity believed in that, too. The difference was that, where God inspired the Christian to voluntary acts of selflessness and sacrifice—acts opposite of his nature—Communism dictated them.

And who decided which one was needy? And which one should meet his needs? The Communist Party hierarchy. All power gravitated to them, and they were loathe to let any of it go. They used it to reward loyal underlings, and they used fear to control any who were suspected of being less than loyal.

Power meant control, and they meant to control every aspect of life, beginning with how and what the children were taught. It might be too late to change the parents, but if they could have the children....

And so, in school the children were taught to have faith in man, in his accomplishments and abilities. This ideology bred into them a primitive desire to satisfy all their inner attitudes, if the opportunity ever presented itself. Which it did, to those steadfastly loyal to the Party. And this was in *every* school, in every village, every company, every organization.

Under the Communists, mediocrity, not merit, was rewarded. The factory worker, the shift supervisor, the plant manager—no one was promoted according to the quality of his work, or his discipline, or his honesty. If he was loyal to the Party, if he was opposed to the faith, if he was perfectly obedient to his superiors, he would rise in the system. No matter that the system destroyed all initiative. No matter that it brought out the worst in men (as the saying went: they pretend to pay us, and we pretend to work). It secured the hierarchy in power.

The Church posed the only threat. At first, they simply killed the priests. In Hercegovina alone, sixty-nine Franciscans were murdered. Most of the others, especially those whose example encouraged the people to keep the faith, were thrown into prison, for anywhere from a few months to fifteen years. Yet still they dared not attack the Church openly; there were still too many faithful.

So they harassed and intimidated and deceived. They searched for a few priests and even bishops who were willing to compromise, and it was amazing what the prospect of a limitless sentence, with months in solitary confinement and possible torture, could do to one's resolve.

The priests who would not compromise, found new meaning in the words of Jesus: *He who would lose his life for my sake, will gain it. But he who would keep his life will lose it.*

And, as always when there is great adversity, the Church thrived. Some priests spent nights sleeping in trees near their churches, so they could not be taken unawares. The people took care of their priests. An old lady told me that in those post-war years you did not give a live chicken to a priest, for it would only be stolen. You cooked it for him and took it to him late at night. And with others in your parish, you organized the care and feeding of your priest.

If you were caught, you would, of course, be imprisoned and possibly even killed. The threat was always there. When you realized what your faith could cost you, then you had to ask yourself: was it worth it?

Many decided that it was. They gave their faith a far higher priority than it had had before—the highest priority.

Satan is the author of fear, and the ultimate weapon in his arsenal is fear of death. Once the Christian loses his fear of death, then the enemy has lost his last hold on him, and he becomes dangerous indeed!

The fear was still there; it was real. But the people learned to live with it. They knew God was with them. So even though they were fearful, they refused to let the fear dictate their lives; they acted heroically.

Every time we let fear decide for us, instead of obedience to the Gospel, we accomplish nothing of value. The absolute fear by which the Communists controlled our country is lessening now, as their grip is loosened. But much fear remains. It is the legacy which they have left us—and the last means of intimidation left to those still in power.

Never again, it is hoped—and prayed—will the Communists regain ascendency. But they have left behind a wasteland in the minds of so many—a tragic legacy of wounded spirits and attitudes towards work and life and each other perhaps permanently crippled.

Americans do not fear their Government, but they are not immune from fear. It is there—fear of forgiving, fear of sacrifice, fear of losing approval, fear of giving.... Fear makes weak Christians. But if in spite of the fear, we do what we know is right, then we do the work of God—heroic deeds.

That was what happened in Hercegovina. The Communist persecution may have intimidated some and caused them to collaborate with their persecutors, but in many others it brought out the best.

And so, as the completion of my studies approached, I came to see that this vocation carried with it far more than was ever imagined. That young boy, playing soccer with his friends who at the last moment changed his mind and decided to become a priest instead of a mechanic—what would he have done, had he known....

God, in His infinite mercy, sometimes spares us from too much knowledge of the future. Especially when we are embarking on a life course which He has laid out for us.

If you are one who some time ago committed your life to His service, look back to when you made that commitment, or chose to deepen it: what would you have done, had you known the trials that awaited? Or the details of the sacrifices which would be required of you?

And yet, at each step, has He not provided the grace necessary to that step? Have you not been thrilled on those occasions, when He has let you know that He is pleased with you? And did you ever know before, the peace that comes from being settled in your vocation?

The whole tree is contained in the seed. The blueprint for its limbs and roots—how many there will be, and where they will go—is known only to God. But it *is* there—all the potential future is contained in the moment of the seed.

It is present, but it is not pre-destined. God may have one tree in mind; we another.

We first have to realize that His plan is better than ours. Then, what sort of tree we become depends entirely upon our step-by-step cooperation with Him. From the tilling of the soil to the planting of the seed, to the nurturing of the tiny shoot, to the watering of the sapling, to the painful pruning of the limbs that they might bring forth more and sweeter fruit... at each step our cooperation is crucial. Without it, the tree will wither. It may become bent or barren. It can even die.

The secret is trust. When we know His will, we must cooperate. Trust—and obey.

So, at seminary I was learning more than just science and history and mathematics. And sometimes my Teacher seemed to delight in instructing me in the most unexpected classrooms. Classrooms which, He knew, would delight me, too—like America.

# 6

# America

In Hercegovina, it was the custom for every candidate for ordination to complete his final year of theological studies abroad. For a Franciscan priest, fluency in another language was essential, and only so much could be absorbed in a classroom. Most of my classmates were going to Italy or Germany, but the country I longed to go to was America.

I had an aunt in America. Our country is so poor that there is, and always has been, a desire among our young people to leave. Few actually do, but most at one time or another dream of it. Nevertheless, in each generation, in each family in each village, there is someone, somewhere, far away.

In the 1920's my aunt married a man, also from our village, who had gone to America previously. They lived near Youngstown, Ohio, and occasionally she would send us gifts and sometimes money—always, it seemed, when we most needed it. It was God's providence, and though I had never met an American and knew little about it beyond what everyone knew, I developed a great love for America.

When God grants us the desire of our heart, it is not just because we have asked Him for it. He gives it to us, if it coincides with His plan for our life. When our desire aligns with His will, great is our joy. (Yet who is to say that He did not plant that desire in the first place?)

And sometimes the reality of what we desire turns out to be quite different from our dream of it. What had I dreamed of? A nation of generous people. A nation who came across the ocean to free Europe, who were today the great, shining alternative to Communism. Everyone of my parents' generation who had met an American soldier said that Americans were big-hearted and sincere. And at seminary, my professors had assured me that the Church was strong in America. So, with no specifics but a rosy picture of the land in which I would complete my theological training, I entered the next stage of the pilgrimage.

Much of America was as I imagined it—but that was not the side of America in which our Church from home was involved. And until I got there, I had no idea how much work there was to be done. So many Croatians had left our country that in every major metropolis, not just in America but throughout Western Europe and South Africa, there was a significant number of my countrymen. In New York, for instance, St Cyril & Methodius Croatian Church numbered some four thousand families. They lived in Connecticut and New Jersey, as well as New York State, and for some it was extremely difficult to get to church on Sunday. But they came.

Often, for newly-arrived Croatian immigrants, the Church provided the only sense of community, the only tie with the family traditions of the old country. Suppose you had just arrived in New York, barely able to speak the language. You were optimistic but scared; it had taken all your courage to come, and practically all your money. You had a cousin there, perhaps, and you were able to get a low-paying job (low pay by American standards was still high pay in our country) and a place to stay. But what about friends? What about people who spoke your language and cared about the things you cared about? What about faith?

The Church in Hercegovina, in Croatia, felt a responsibility to these far-flung people, to continue to provide for them what she always had: an identity, a stability, a spiritual and moral focus. With that foundation for their new life, they would become good Americans—Croatian-Americans, secure in their cultural traditions, with an abiding faith which they would pass on to their children. The children would have much less difficulty adapting to their new country, fitting into the local church wherever they moved, but their parents' needs were immediate and pressing. To meet them, the Church needed everyone who could help.

After completing my theological training in Washington, D.C, I was ordained a priest at St Stanislav's Church in Chicago in 1977. My first assignment (of three years) was working with Croatian immigrants in Milwaukee. There I came to see that the concept of being an immigrant was common to all Americans, whether it was a few years or a few generations old. The "melting pot," far from dissolving a newcomer's personality, become a receptacle and a point of exchange: in return for the great blessing of the new world, he gave it the best he had brought with him from the old.

At the end of summer of 1980, I was assigned to St Cyril's in New York. At 10th Avenue and 41st Street, St Cyril's was a magnificent old church in a run-down section of the inner city. It could hold 1500 people, and on Sundays we could have used half again as many pews.

The pastor was Fr. Slavko Soldo, like myself a Croatian from the mountains of Hercegovina. I liked this man very much, not just because his village back home was less than two hours from my own, but because he possessed an ideal balance of wisdom and humor, commitment and hard work. God chooses His shepherds well, and there could not have been a better choice for St Cyril's.

Sensitive to the need of his flock for a feeling of belonging, he organized church picnics and other family activities that would bring people together, and periodically he made pastoral calls to their homes. New York can be a forbidding place, a place where one can easily become suddenly, deeply lonely. The door to the past might be closed, but the door to the Church was open.

The first Christmas in New York was memorable. St Cyril's had a large downstairs hall, and after Mass almost everyone went down there for a social time. They would stay sometimes for a couple of hours, as many had come a long way, and this was the center of their week. On Christmas Day, since it was such a happy time and so important to families, they stayed even longer. At last, all had left but three young men, talking together in a corner. I went over to them and said, "I'm sorry, but we have to close the church now, so I'm afraid you are going to have to leave."

One of them turned on me and burst out: "Father, where would you have us go? Today is Christmas, but we have no families here—no brothers, sisters, parents. So, where would you have us go? To bars? To the streets or empty rooms?"

Looking into his eyes, I could feel what he was feeling. "You stay here as long as you like," I said, and for the next several hours we shared our destinies.

In the gritty streets of the west side of mid-town Manhattan, God was teaching His young priest about reality. And for reasons known only to Him, it was imperative that the student learn—and grow up—quickly. So the lessons in this new classroom were difficult and demanding.

I did not realize how far the reality of my new surroundings differed from my imagined ideal, until the first time I ventured to Times Square. Before World War II, Times Square, where Broadway met 7th Avenue at 44th Street, was portrayed as the glamorous center of New York City, and to middle Europe, New York was the most glamorous city in the Western World. Movies from America painted the most romantic vision of Times Square, and while that legend was badly tarnished by the time I arrived in New

York, still I was curious. So one evening after supper, leaving my robe in the closet of my room in the rectory, I decided to walk the streets of New York.

At first, Times Square was what I had once imagined—tall buildings (tall to me), bright lights, much traffic, sidewalks crowded with people in a hurry. And above them, huge billboards (bigger than I could have imagined), announced new movies or products. It was breathtaking, and I could see that once, when the world was younger, this might indeed have been the most exciting place it had to offer.

But in the half-century which had passed since then, the world had lost its innocence. There had been a world-wide Depression, a world-wide war, a world-wide epidemic of Communism, a worldwide epidemic of drugs and disease—of the mind, as well as the body. And of the soul: the influence of faith upon mankind was waning, while the lure of the world was growing steadily stronger.

Faith was grounded in reality, beginning with the reality that there was no good thing in man, save Christ and Him crucified.

Without Christ, man's base instinct was to serve himself, if necessary at the expense of others.

God had made man in His image, but with Adam's sin, man had lost his innocence, his purity. Now, he needed God to save him from his nature.

He needed God to cleanse and purify him, to renew and inspire him.

The world, and the prince of this planet, dealt in unreality. He lied now, just as he had in the Garden. And he was telling man the same lie: man did not need God; he did not need anyone but himself. He should please himself always, starting with the sweet taste of the fruit of the knowledge of good and evil. That knowledge would make him like God. God did not want to share that knowledge with man, so God had lied to him, telling him that if he ate of that fruit, he would die.

This was the lie the serpent told, and the first man had chosen to believe him, rather than God. He ate of the fruit, and his innocence died. Because we are accountable for what we do, God had no choice but to banish man from the Garden.

But He still loved His creation, and through one prophet after another He called man back to Himself. Sometimes man would listen, and his heavenly Father would bless him. And then man would forget again.

Finally, He sent His only begotten Son, to redeem mankind, once and for all. It worked—enough men heard. The faith spread around the world.

But now, as we neared the end of the second millennium, it seemed that once again more men were listening to the serpent than to God. And the serpent was spinning a web of fantasy. This needle, this drink, this act, this relationship—will erase your unhappiness. You will have relief from pain, from anguish, from fear. You will know peace. There is dirt in this world, to be sure; it is a dark place, but it is an exciting place. And it holds happiness for you; soon you will have all you desire. And be rid of all you dislike.

Times Square offered all of these things—openly, blatantly. Drugs, pornography, prostitution—whatever your secret craving, it could be satisfied there. For those who were buying, the price was minimal.

But it was costing them their souls; you could see it in their eyes.

The farther I walked into that world, the more mired in its quicksand I became. And then suddenly I was assaulted by all the combined evil of this world. It was overwhelming. I felt like there were hands in my mind, groping for me, clawing at me. I could not pray; I could not even think. It was all I could do to turn around and start walking back.

The blocks seemed to take forever, and all the while the hands kept reaching. I had to concentrate just to keep walking. Finally I was back in my room, exhausted and feeling defeated. But in a war, sometimes just by staying alive, you win a victory. You come home bleeding; your arms and legs are broken, your head wounded. But you are still alive. You reach your home, and you have a chance to recover.

I began to pray. The surrounding of the good people in the rectory, the strong building itself, and the prayers—all of these combined to create a holy environment. God was there. Hope was there. And gradually the filth which I had encountered was scraped away. In future years, looking back on that episode, it would occur to me that perhaps the greatest victory of my life was won that night.

There were other encounters with reality, as God continued to teach me how little I could do to alter my environment, and how foolish I was to try to do so in my own strength. St Cyril's was located in an area where there was much crime. One night around three o' clock, I awoke with the awareness that someone was in my room. I could see the silhouette against the open window, where he must have come in. I jumped out of bed, and he ran away, but he could not have been any more scared than I was.

The very next day, Friday, in the evening we had a young people's gathering. We had some practice, a little prayer, and then some entertainment. It was almost midnight when it was finished.

I closed up the hall and started walking to the rectory, just a few steps away, when two young men tried to mug me. I didn't have any money, but that didn't stop them.

In the following month our church was robbed ten times. After they had taken the chalices, there was little of value, but they kept coming back. One day, I went to use the sound system, and the speakers were gone. One night they even stole the cans of soda, stored in the basement for our next picnic.

One afternoon, I was making the rounds of the church and discovered a man on the roof of the hall, trying to make a hole to enter. I called the police, but he ran away before they could come. I grabbed a piece of wood, and not knowing what to do, ran this way and that. Seeing me, Fr. Slavko shook his head and sadly exclaimed, "Fr. Svet fights the crime of New York!"

Those were sad times. I was trying to do everything, taking it all on my shoulders. It was quicksand of a different kind, but quicksand, nonetheless: the more you struggled, the deeper you sank.

And God let me make the mistakes, so that in the future I would never forget what I was learning.

I learned that I could always pray. And that He was always there to hear me, to take my confession and forgive me, to give me the grace I needed for each day.

If I asked, He would guide me. He would give me the wisdom that I lacked, the courage that I needed. But each time I had to ask.

I learned that with prayer, not only could I change my own outlook—and help others to change theirs. And bit by bit I was sorting out the things that were part of a priest's call—the things he should do himself, and what he should allow others to do. If a priest was obedient in carrying out his assignment, then his time would be full, and he would have peace. And be a source of peace for others.

What I was learning, of course, had been summed up by the founder of our order in this simple prayer: *God, grant me the courage to change what I can change, the patience to accept what I can not change, and the wisdom to know the difference.*

One day, at lunch in the rectory towards the end of June, 1981, God gave the first hint of what my next classroom would be, though I did not recognize it as such.

Fr. Slavko, sitting at the head of the long wooden table, said, "You know, I have heard the most amazing story from home! Six children there have seen the Blessed Virgin Mary. And she is returning to them every day! To my village, Medjugorje. Imagine!"

From the moment he said it, I knew in my heart that it was true.

# 7

# Home

The Blessed Virgin Mary was appearing in Medjugorje! I could not take it out of my mind! Such a thing had happened at Fatima, Portugal, in 1917, and at Lourdes in the previous century. There, the apparitions occurred for only a short time. If what Fr. Slavko had heard was true, she was continuing to return to all six of the young people from his village at the same time every afternoon—day after day, week after week!

*Was* it true? For some reason, it never occurred to me to doubt it. Perhaps because I was from the same mountains in Hercegovina. I knew our people, young and old: they could not create such a hoax. It was authentic.

And I felt compelled to do whatever possible to spread the word of what was happening there.

Why wasn't it on the front page of the newspapers? At the top of the television news? Frantically I pieced together the fragments of different accounts into a coherent report, and contacted the newspapers to give them the story. They listened, but only out of politeness. Yes, Father, well, that's very interesting, but it really doesn't sound like something for our readership. Perhaps in your diocesan newsletter....

How will they respond, I wondered, when the Lord Himself returns? Perhaps they will find room for that story after the baseball scores.

Meanwhile, my appetite for each scrap of news of the apparitions was insatiable. Was there a visitor in our church who had just come from home? Had they heard what was happening in Medjugorje? They must tell me! Their account would be added to my growing notebook. In the process, I discovered how far away Medjugorje was from New York—far enough for some stories to get twisted en route.

So I was careful about what went into the notebook, especially what was marked "Confirmed."

Fr. Slavko was becoming concerned. It wasn't that I was neglecting other duties; it was just that Medjugorje was all I could think or talk about. "Sveto, it's *my* home! But you don't see me carrying on the way you are!" He shook his head. "I fear you are becoming obsessed!"

If so, it was a divine obsession. Too often, I seemed to be in the right place at the right time to hear the right story, for me to doubt that God was helping.

It was not the apparitions themselves that had so galvanized me: it was what *Gospa* (the Blessed Mother) was *saying*. For she was telling the young people (who were already being referred to as the visionaries) that the reason she had come was to call all men back to God. Essentially her messages came down to this: she was calling for conversion. For people to put God ahead of all else in their lives and to live only to

do His will. Always, she was pointing people to her
Son, saying to all who would listen, the same thing
which she had said at the Wedding Feast in Cana: "Do
as He tells you."

The way to conversion, she explained—and from
there to forgiveness and reconciliation— was through
prayer. And fasting. And penance, which was doing
selfless acts of love, where one might once have behaved selfishly. These were the messages of Medjugorje—the messages that I was so anxious, almost
desperate, to disseminate.

And suddenly, in the midst of all my activity, I realized that I had never known such happiness.

Does God sometimes plant the desire of our heart
in our heart? Until this moment, nothing in my life
had held this importance. Indeed, it seemed as if my
life had been waiting for Medjugorje to happen.

It never occurred to me to ask God to one day be
assigned there; that would be to ask the impossible. I
was content to help right there in New York. Besides,
with 10,000 parishioners there was more than three
priests could handle at St Cyril' s, as it was.

In the summer of 1982, after five years in America, it
was time for me to take home leave. At the beginning
of August, I would fly to Zagreb, and spend 45 days in
my beloved mountains, visiting my family. And while
there, a visit to Medjugorje might be possible.

In those days, going home was not an easy decision
to make. There could be trouble with the Government.

For the doors of St Cyril's were open to all worshippers, regardless of their politics—and that included exiled dissidents. To control the different peoples of Yugoslavia, the Communists used fear, and they had a wide variety of sophisticated methods of applying it. One was the threat of exile. Someone causing trouble who traveled abroad, or who spoke against the Government while abroad, might find himself forbidden to return. To never be allowed home again, not even when your mother or father was dying, was enough of a threat to close the mouth of the most outspoken critic.

But what of those who *were* shut out? What of those forced to remain in America? Were they to be shut out of our church, too? Of course not! In their loneliness, we often became their family away from home. Sometimes they would be verbally bitter about the Communists—and they would be heard; even in America the Secret Police had their agents. They had their lists of names, and there was little doubt that the priests who served at St Cyril's were listed there. Certainly we were aware of being observed and followed.

I was not afraid of being shut out; my parents had both died. The only thing they could do to me was shut me in—allow me to enter and then revoke my passport or imprison me.

While I had joined no conspiracies, no demonstrations, and had never spoken out against the Government, nevertheless there was little doubt that my private sympathies were known to them. And so there was a fear of the system which had the technique to break the mind and will of those whom it considered its opponents.

It was all right to be afraid, as long as you didn't let your fear make your decision. It was time to go home.

When the plane landed in Zagreb, the line for passport control seemed to be moving well—*nema problema,* as the young people from home were fond of saying. But standing before the counter, all that changed. The official examined my passport for a long time, then asked his superior to come over. The superior examined it, then went to get his superior. At that point I had real fear; this had not happened to anyone else.

Most countries treated traveling priests with friendly courtesy—even respect, if the immigration agent happened to be Catholic. That was not going to happen here. In my country the State regarded the Church as its enemy. Now, one of the Church's most junior officers had fallen into their hands. And his name was on the list.

Soon we were in a small private office, where for the next four hours I was interrogated. You might wonder what questions could possibly take four hours to ask. I wondered, too. It seemed like they hadn't really figured out what to ask. But I had to be suspect, or my name would not have been on the list. Gradually I came to realize that the questions were not important; it was the humiliation. They were impressing upon me that I was not in America now; I was in their country. And I was theirs, to do with as they wished.

Suddenly they released me. No apology, no explanation. "You're free to go now," the interrogating officer yawned, dismissing me without looking up. "But we'll keep this," he smiled up at me, picking up my passport and dropping it into a desk drawer.

Most people will never know what it is like to leave such an office and walk the streets of the city which is the heart of your country... for the moment, you and the city are free. But over you both is a shadow which could fall at any moment and envelop you in darkness.

I shuddered and felt cold, though it was still summer. And then in the distance I saw four nuns walking towards me. Their black habits swirled in the late afternoon wind. They were cheerful, oblivious to the oppression I had just left. The sight of them was a welcoming word: You are home. And I am here.

I walked on, and eventually came to the great cathedral of Zagreb. Its doors were open, and as I approached, its bells started to ring. They were like a mother's hands reaching out to receive me. I went up the steps and entered. The interior was dark, save for a shaft of sunlight coming through a stained-glass window. I went over to the tomb of Cardinal Stepinac, who had died while under house arrest in 1962. His story was known to all of us, and now it was as if God was saying to me: "Walk with courage, my son; he walked the same path. You will not go alone."

When I reached my brother's house in Kocerin, he was glad to see me, but he was also worried. The *Milicija* (police) had already been there. "They want you to come to their headquarters in Mostar tomorrow, ten o'clock." He looked at me. "Sveto, are you in trouble?"

"Not that I am aware of," I replied casually, forcing a smile. "But I will have to borrow your car."

At dinner we tried to be festive—it was my first night home in three years.

Actually it seemed even longer, for I had seldom seen them, when I was in seminary, and now there were two more children in the family. I told them stories of America, and they told me what my nieces and nephews were doing and the rest of our relatives. But behind the laughter, there was concern. As the *Milicija* knew there would be. Just as they knew I would come to their headquarters without an escort and would be on time. Because otherwise, it might cause trouble for my brother and his family. That was why they had come to him in person, rather than using the phone or the mail. It was all part of the intimidation.

That night I prayed and confessed my fear to God. He knew it already, of course, but He also knew it would be good for me to hear myself confessing it to Him. Then He reminded me who was the author of fear. I knew it was Satan, of course, but it was good to be reminded. Then He asked me who was stronger, He or the enemy. And Who was still on His throne. And Who would go with me tomorrow, each step of the way. And give me the words I needed, just before I needed them.

I felt better after that.

At 10 o'clock the following morning, I presented myself at *Milicija* headquarters. Soon I was in another small room, facing two other interrogators across a desk. This time, however, there was a point to their questions: Did I know so-and-so?

What, how could I not be sure? I was seen with him on April 17, 1981, at such-and-such a place. And had I not invited him to a church supper on May 8? Had I not told him that I would pray for his family and make a special intention of the Mass for his mother, who was having heart trouble?

Even as they ask such questions, you start wondering who their informer is. Let's see, only two people knew that...

Pretty soon you are in an attitude of paranoia—which is what they want. Everyone is spying on you; you can't trust anyone, and so on. You are alone, and they are so many.

Plus, their information is so accurate that you soon find yourself believing that it's hopeless: they already know everything anyway, apparently even what you are thinking. So what is the point of hiding or denying anything?

But I realized that this, too, was part of the technique of intimidation. So I continued to say as little as possible.

This time, something else was different: the interrogation had a definite goal, beyond humiliation. They had a paper they wanted me to sign. It stated that I had done certain things, that I apologized for them, and that I would not do them again. If I signed it, they would not bother me again. I could come and go as I liked, and I could return to America at the end of my stay. If I did not sign it—the chief interrogator tapped my passport which was now on this desk, next to the paper—I would never see my passport again.

The paper contained nothing particularly damaging; I had opened the church to known dissidents, hostile to the government of the Socialist Federal Republic of Yugoslavia. But while the charges themselves might not be that serious, the act of signing the paper was. If I signed, I might go free physically—but I would have to live for the rest of my life with the knowledge that I had signed it.

And that was what my interrogators wanted: to destroy my self-respect. It did not even matter to them if, when I returned to America, I continued to open the church to dissidents. They would know, and I would know, that I had signed the paper. Priests, because they had no wives or children, were more difficult to control. But if you could get one to sign a confession, it was like an act of contrition; after that, he belonged to you, no matter what he did.

So I did not sign. Four hours became five, and then six. They finally let me go, but they indicated that they would have me back. And they did, the following week, for another all-day session. And the week after that, and the week after that. Never on the same day of the week, never at the same time. And always notifying me through a personal visit to a member of my family.

At this point I must emphasize that I was no hero. I would not sign the paper, but I was in fear most of the time. Nor was what was happening to me in any way unique. The same thing had happened to thousands of my countrymen, and most suffered far worse treatment at their hands than I did. Many were imprisoned. Many of those were tortured. Some were martyred.

After each interrogation I would report to my superior, the Provincial in Mostar, responsible for all the

Franciscans in Hercegovina. I related to him in detail what had taken place, and what I had said. Each time he approved of my actions and offered me encouragement. I was sorry to be such a bother to him, but how grateful I was to be able to go to him! It was not a good time to be alone.

One wonderful thing did happen during that home leave. About a week after my arrival, my biggest wish came true: I went to Medjugorje!

# 8

# Medjugorje

For my first visit to Medjugorje, I decided to go anonymously, without wearing my robe. Just a pilgrim, walking into the village from Citluk. It was late in the afternoon, but going quickly, I could cover the six kilometers in time for the six o' clock Mass. Before the Mass, as the visionaries said the rosary, she would come.

Approaching the turn-off for Medjugorje, I noticed the man in the white helmet, standing in the middle of the intersection, with his white motorcycle parked beside him. He was stopping each vehicle, each pedestrian, questioning them. In those days, the Government was not happy with the apparitions and the pilgrims they were attracting. How could a system whose ideology declared there was no God, condone the continuing appearances of His mother?

The Government had done everything possible to stop the apparitions. They had forbidden the children from going up the hill where she had first appeared, because thousands had been gathering there, some driving for hours. They had interrogated the children at police headquarters, grilling them separately as if they were criminals, trying to break their story. They had examined them in a hospital by state psychiatrists, attempting to certify that they were insane, or at least suffering delusions. They had tried to intimidate their families — and their pastor, Fr. Jozo Zovko, and two other priests of the Franciscan community there, Fr. Ferdo Vlasic and Fr. Jozo Krizic. When they refused to denounce the apparitions, the Communists had thrown them into prison where they continued to try to break them.

When nothing succeeded, they started harassing the pilgrims. They would fly their helicopters low over the church, right in the middle of the worship, and would drive their police cars ominously through the village at all hours of the day and night. At the airports and border crossings, Customs agents would confiscate pilgrims' Bibles, rosaries, and other religious articles.

In later years, when it finally dawned on them what a million pilgrims each year was doing for the regional economy, they reversed their position, scrambling to build hotels as fast as possible. But in the summer of '82, they were still harassing the pilgrims — with checkpoints like the one which now awaited me.

In sandals, with my pack slung over my shoulder, I may have looked like a pilgrim, but when the *Milicija* officer heard me speak, he would know I was a local. That could work in my favor; he might just assume that I lived nearby and was walking home from work.

The only danger was my pack. In it, in addition to a camera and a little tape-recorder, were letters from friends in America to relatives at home. If for any reason he found them suspicious and used his radio, he would discover that I had been interrogated at *Milicija* headquarters in both Zagreb and Mostar. Then the camera and the tape-recorder could become sinister, and the letters could contain code. And I could find myself on my way to Mostar again, this time with an escort.

I had not yet approached closely enough for him to notice me. He was busy checking the identity papers—identity papers! I had none! My passport was at *Milicija* headquarters!

I slowed and started to turn around. I could still walk away, unnoticed. Perhaps later I could get there by crossing pastures and going through the woods....

But fear was not going to make this decision. I was going to Medjugorje. My heart was set on it—in fact, it was on fire to go there! So I would face whatever needed to be faced to get there.

I walked up to the officer, who asked my name and where I was from. (There was no need to ask where I was going.) The moment he heard my accent, he smiled and started to wave me past, more interested in the Mercedes sedan which was approaching. Then he noticed my pack.

"What is in there?" he asked, nodding at it.

"A few personal things," I shrugged, "nothing important."

"Open it."

I slipped the pack off my shoulder and held it open for him.

"And these?" he pointed at the envelopes.

"Letters to friends, from America."

He looked at me, his eyes narrowing. "You're from America?"

I nodded.

"Occupation?"

"I'm a priest, home for a visit."

He looked over at the radio on the motorcycle, but just then another Mercedes drew up behind the first one, and a taxi came behind it. He picked an envelope. "Open this one," he directed.

I did, and he read it.

"Well," he said hesitantly, returning the letter to its envelope, "you may go."

I thanked him and walked up the turn-off. It was paved but narrow; two cars could barely pass without one getting part way off to let the other by. (Back then, the massive tourist buses had not yet begun to arrive.)

The sun was low on my right, when I first caught sight of St James Church, familiar from many grainy pictures. I almost stopped to take a picture, but I did not want to miss any more of the Mass than I had to. I realized that I was behaving like a child on Christmas morning and reminded myself that I was 31 years old. Then I shrugged and gave in to it—I *was* like a child... on the first Christmas... going to Bethlehem... to see the Son and His mother.

When I crossed the little brook and turned sharply right, the church was directly before me, its twin spires now silhouetted in the gathering twilight. As I got closer, I strained to hear what they were singing—*Dosli smo ti Majko Draga,* the hymn of Medjugorje which I had heard on tape, back in New York. Grinning, I picked up the pace, humming with them as I went.

Where the paved road swung left, a dirt path led right up to the steps of the church. (Today, in place of the dirt parking area, there is a magnificent stone plaza, stretching more than a hundred meters.) I walked to the foot of the steps and looked up at the heavy arched doors. When the church had been built in 1966, for some reason the villagers had made it twice as large as their population needed. Now, of course, they knew why.

With reverence I slowly went up the steps. The doors were open; the church was full. Every seat was taken; there were even people standing in the aisles. I went over to the right wall and went forward as far as I could. Outwardly I may have been silent, anonymous, but inside, my emotions were so powerful I felt like a bomb was about to go off at any moment!

The Mass ended, and the rosary began. The young visionaries were in the sacristy, through the small door to the right of the altar.

All at once, the praying stopped. The one whose prayers we were requesting had come. In the sacristy, unseen by the congregation, the visionaries were conversing with her.

I strained to hear something, anything, but could not. Nor did I see anything. But I did feel something — great peace. And an overwhelming joy at being allowed to be a part of this work, however small. At that moment I knew — not with my head but in my heart — that this was what I wanted to devote my life to. That, of course, was not for a priest to decide. Priests did not pick their assignments; they were assigned.

Afterwards, I went over to the rectory next to the church, where the priests of Medjugorje were. Franciscans like myself, two were from Hercegovina and known to me, including St James' new pastor, Tomislav Pervan. I had decided to ask permission to actually meet one or more of the visionaries. After all, I thought, when would I ever come back to Medjugorje? This would be my only opportunity to meet them, and I might always regret not having tried. So I asked one of the priests: "Um, could it possibly be arranged for me to speak with the visionaries? "

"Why ask me?" he replied. "Just go and see them yourself."

That was a revelation; I had assumed that the priests were supervising the visionaries. It had never occurred to me that they were completely independent; in fact, they were not even sure where the visionaries were.

I was even more surprised—stunned—a few minutes later, when all six of the young people suddenly arrived at the rectory. No one had sent for them; no one was expecting them. Fr. Pervan introduced me, and they accepted me immediately. It was more than acceptance; it was as if we had known each other all our lives. At first, I assumed it was because I was from Hercegovina, but later I had the sense that there was more to it than that. I decided to stop assuming anything.

Coincidence or not, I was not going to waste this extraordinary opportunity. I asked if they would mind my interviewing them, and they did not mind a bit.

Ivanka, Mirjana, and Ivan had to go home, but Vicka, Marija, and Jacov joined me in a little room. I turned on my tape-recorder and asked them every question I could think of—which was not too many; how I wished I'd had the opportunity to prepare proper questions! As it was, it did not take long, and we all enjoyed it. Later, I could not find that tape (and to this day I do not know what became of it), but it didn't matter; I had stored it all up in my heart.

The main thing was, these were perfectly normal and very likeable young people. They were not at all spoiled as a result of all the attention they were getting, though privately they sometimes wished it would all go away. But not the Blessed Mother! They loved her and looked forward to her coming each day. She asked them to pray with her for the lost souls and the unconverted, for peace in the world, for young people like themselves. She had told them there would be many pilgrims, and for them to be loving to them, because in coming to Medjugorje, many would come—or come back—to God.

Then they had to leave, and I knew it was time for me to, also. I walked back to Citluk in a daze. I had just spoken and laughed with three young people who had prayed and spoken with the Mother of God. And they did this every day. And I was not dreaming or hallucinating.

I looked up at the night sky, at the stars that were lighting my way. God had put them there. He had set each one in place, had established the orbits of the planets circling them, had set each planet spinning on its axis. And now, to this little village, he had sent the one mortal whose obedience had been perfect.

She had wanted to come. From the moment her Son, even as He hung on the Cross, had given John—and all men—to her, she had loved all mankind, as if they were her own children.

Would they listen to her? They were not listening to His anointed servants. He had poured out His Spirit upon all flesh, and even that, with all its attendant miracles and healing, had not been sufficient to cause men to turn back to Him. Perhaps now they would listen to His mother. Time would tell. But there was little time left.

There was little time left for me in Hercegovina. All too soon the 45 days were up, and I was due to go back to New York. But before I could leave, there was one more interrogation—this one was the longest and the hardest yet. Hour after hour, my interrogator went over the known facts of what I had done, adding to them places and times and circumstances of meetings which had occurred during my home leave. Over and over the material he went, until we were both emotionally drained, exhausted, our nerves raw.

Finally he leaned back in his chair. "You are planning to fly back to New York tomorrow morning, are you not?"

I nodded.

"You realize that you will not be on that plane, if you don't sign this paper."

I said nothing.

"You will never fly anywhere again!"

I just looked at him.

He slammed the desktop with his hand. "Whether or not we put you in prison," he exploded, "you will be our prisoner! You will not even be able to cross the street without our permission! Do you understand that? Do you understand what I am saying?"

I understood. I also understood that somehow, after Medjugorje, the menace of this interrogation was not the same. It was as if the stinger of the wasp had been drawn.

At last he said to me quietly:

"You are not going to sign, are you."

"No."

"Then take a good look at this!" he exclaimed, his hand trembling as he held up my passport, "because you will never see it again!"

He shoved back his chair and stood up. "This interview is concluded."

With a sigh I got to my feet. "I am free to go?"

"For now," he nodded, sighing himself. Then, with a smile—the first time he had smiled all day—he opened the door for me.

He walked out with me, as if we were friends, and I sensed that he was as relieved as I was that it was finally over. At the front door, he put a hand on my arm and looked me in the eye. His eyes were pleading. "You don't have to do this, you know. Please, it's not worth it; you're giving up too much."

For a moment I almost nodded. All day long I had resisted, but now it was over, and my guard was down. And he was appealing to me, as a friend who had been through a great ordeal with me.

He was practically begging.

I opened my mouth to speak, when the thought came: how many others have broken at this moment?

I shook my head.

He sighed again. "Perhaps we could get together sometime, maybe have a meal in a restaurant somewhere."

And now I did speak: "If you would like me to see you, you can summon me to your office here, and I will come. But nowhere else."

I turned and walked down the steps. I was their prisoner, perhaps—but I felt more free than I ever had in my life.

I grinned; I was God's prisoner now. And I wondered what He had in store for me.

# 9

# Konjic

When the Provincial learned that he now had another priest on his hands, one with whom the *Milicija* were none too happy, he knew just where to send me: "You will go to the monastery of Humac, in Ljubuski. They are short of priests there."

Ljubuski was only 15 kilometers from Medjugorje! And my duties at the monastery were minimal. I was regularly scheduled for only one Mass every day and two on Sundays, and two hours of religious instruction a week; the rest of my time was completely free, to do with as I wished. With Medjugorje so near, it is not hard to imagine how I spent it. When the other friars would sympathize with me for having lost such a wonderful assignment as New York, I would nod, long-faced, not letting on how thrilled I was to be there. They helped with clothing and other needs, for everything had been left in New York—a whole world had been left behind, for the new world to begin.

There were hardly any English-speaking pilgrims coming to Medjugorje in 1982, just a few pioneers. But they were preparing the way for countless thousands who would follow them. It was obvious that there was work to be done, to prepare for the coming of the future pilgrims and to provide the sound and basic information that they would need. This was the time to learn about the calling that was coming, and many days were spent studying—it was like being back in university. Far from lamenting the loss of the passport, there was only joy, as God prepared me for this new calling.

Everything that happened—everything that happens—is God's providence. It might be glorious, like health restored, or it might be a seeming loss, like having a passport revoked. For those who courageously recognize God's hand in it, it will work for good in their lives.

One day I was talking with one of the sisters who had been serving there from the beginning, when she happened to mention that Fr. Jozo had interviewed the visionaries extensively before he had been arrested. Did he by any chance tape the interviews? Yes. What had happened to the tapes? When the *Milicija* had come for him, she had hidden them. Did she still have them? Of course. Might I borrow them? Certainly.

I could not believe this! For months in New York I had scavenged for fragments and second and third-hand scraps of the story. Now, all at once, I was being given the most valuable information in existence! All that needed to be done was to transcribe the tapes and organize the transcripts. Then preface it with a general background, and add perhaps one or two more other interviews....

Never had hard work been so easy! It was almost as if someone had put a pen in my hand and said: Now write! The pen never rested. Neither did the typewriter which I had been given the use of. Why such urgency? I did not know—but everything seemed to be going that way. And so with transcribing and writing and editing and more writing, gradually a manuscript took shape.

It was barely finished in the spring of 1984, when a Franciscan priest, Fr. Michael Scanlan, came over from the University of Steubenville in Ohio, to see for himself what was happening. When he asked if the details and chronology were set down on paper anywhere, I was able to present him with the manuscript.

He took it to America, where it was published by Franciscan Herald Press under the title, *The Apparitions of Our Lady of Medjugorje*. Many people bought it, and the proceeds went towards the building of a mission church, even farther up in the mountains—where I would be going next.

In early October of that year, a new assignment came: to another monastery, high up in the mountains, in Konjic, on the Neretva River, half way to Sarajevo. It was ten times the distance from Medjugorje, and there was ten times as much work to do right there.

At first, it was difficult to understand. Why this? Had I not given my utmost? Was this a reward?

Had someone else, during counseling or confession, asked me those same questions, I would have reminded him (or her) that when a child asks his father for a piece of bread, he does not give him a stone. But the Father can see farther than His child can, and He knows better what is best for him. The thing to remember was that the Father loved him perfectly. He was raising him up in the way He wanted him to go, training him for the future. When you are training a young grapevine, sometimes you must make the limbs go where they do not want to, and you must use your pruning knife, often severely.

But you do love that vine, and you are doing this in order that it will produce the best possible fruit. Of course, to the vine, it may not feel like love, at the time.

Easy to say to someone else—but hard to accept. Especially when the pruning felt like punishment. What I thought was important for me to be doing was not always what my superiors thought was important for me to be doing. Indeed, not since I had become a priest had my vow of obedience cut so deeply.

I had counseled others to trust God in all things, no matter what; now I had to live it. Because the alternative was unthinkable.

Gradually, through painful circumstances and many hard lessons (with me, the lessons never seemed to be easy), I began to learn what it truly meant to go to Konjic. Obedience was better than sacrifice. (Obedience was someone else's idea of what you should sacrifice.) God honors obedience, especially when it is costly. I learned that if you do not like a task, but it is what you are supposed to be doing, then you can ask Him to change your heart, and He will answer that prayer in the twinkling of an eye. (You still may not like it, but you will be content.) One definition of maturity: the ability to postpone pleasure. To trust God through another's authority was difficult, but the only sure way to answer one's calling.

In all these things there was a great deal of growing up to do—in a very short time.

Konjic was the perfect place for that. The monastery had been built in 1939. The Communists had confiscated it in 1946, and when they returned it to the Franciscans in 1970, nothing worked. It was totally run down. When I arrived in 1984, each friar's room did contain a bed, usually broken, and some rooms also had a chair. But none had a table on which to write. And everywhere massive repairs were needed—for which there was no money. In fact, the economy in all of Konjic was a shambles. Our parishioners were working as hard as they could just to survive, and none had the opportunity to give major assistance in rebuilding and renewing the parish.

It was in this critical situation that we truly heard the words of St Francis—words that we had often listened to, without hearing: go out into the world and *build* the Church, spiritually, as well as physically.

Spiritually, there was also much to do. Konjic was the easternmost outpost of Roman Catholicism. As such, it had suffered greatly under the three centuries of Turkish domination.

When the Turks left, the Church came to life again. The main church in Konjic was re-built in 1895. It was a magnificent old structure, majestic yet intimate (despite its being numbingly cold in winter).

I loved serving there. Plus, there were two new mission churches, for parishioners who were too far away to get to the big church in town. Even by 1984, few families had cars, and the mountains there were so steep that bicycles were not much help. So people walked—just as they had when I was a little boy.

I was given responsibility for one of these churches. It was my first church—and you grow up very quickly, when you suddenly have a congregation looking to you for inspiration. Back in New York, Fr. Slavko had taught me by his example what it meant to care for such a flock. I, too, made house calls—and found that the more involved I became with these people's lives, the more I cared for them.

Soon this parish and my work in the monastery was as important to me as my occasional trips down to Medjugorje. And eventually my work in Konjic, and my responsibility to the souls which God had entrusted, was the most important thing. And that, I sensed, pleased God.

It may also have caused Him to smile. For once my outlook had achieved a proper balance, He could trust me to go down to Medjugorje more often. But the moment that going down there became more important than it should be, more important than my primary assignment, then decisions or circumstances would arise that would prevent me from going. It would frustrate me at first, but I soon came to see that this was the common sense that God uses to lead his people. And that it was love.

Years passed. I wrote another book, *In the Company of Mary,* and with the collapse of Communism in the

Eastern Bloc countries, including my country, I was once again issued a passport.

With it I began to be invited to travel abroad, to help spread the message of Medjugorje.

At this point it is important to stop the narrative and say one thing that is necessary: every priest, every friar, every sister, every layperson who has been called to serve the pilgrims in Medjugorje has a story, and the one you are reading is the least important. Consider it as only a symbol. Throughout the history of Hercegovina, there have been numberless servants of God who have glorified Him and lived the truth of the Gospel, without ever being noticed, let alone having anything to do with books.

Medjugorje has been placed in the midst of this rich history of the Church, and depends on no priest or community of priests. It depends equally on all who are called to help, in whatever capacity. And it is this spirit of selfless giving which amplifies the Spirit of God in that place.

The work there is at once simple and complex. No one organizes it, and no one is being organized. Everyone is contributing a little to it. The priests who preach, hear confessions, give counseling, write books, and lead in prayer are doing what they have been called to do. This narrative offers merely a minor facet of that vast mosaic. The people who make the beds, drive the buses, lead the pilgrims, cook the food, make the arrangements, care for the houses—all are part of this mosaic.

I look forward to going down to Medjugorje—but I also look forward to coming back up the Neretva, to home. There is as much work to do in Konjic, but here one also has a chance to pray, to write, and to reflect. It is good to find that one can take this peace down to Medjugorje, where the blessings go in every direction. Sometimes I think of myself as a mailman, bringing a letter which contains the best of monastic life in the mountains—the steady focus on God's presence.

One has to smile at the wisdom of God, in arranging things the way He has. He knows us so much better than we know ourselves. He knows our talents, our dreams—what we need and when we need it. With our trust and sensitive listening in obedience, He will bring out and fulfill the best in us.

# 10

# Pilgrimage

*A pilgrimage is a journey, assigned by God. It brings the pilgrim not only to a physical place, but out of himself, and into the presence of God. All else falls away. There is only the child, his Father, and eternity....*

In ancient times, pilgrimages were made to holy places. As an act of faith, or to renew the relationship they once had with God, or to gain one that others seemed to have, pilgrims journeyed to the traditional sites of the birth, death, and resurrection of Jesus. If that was impossible, they traveled to a shrine or a great cathedral. It might take many days or even weeks to get there, but the distance did not matter; the journey itself was as important as the destination. For it was a preparation and a purification.

Coming to the decision to go—and all that led up to it—was also part of the process. In a sense, the pilgrimage began at the moment it first occurred to the individual that he (or she) might undertake such a venture. It would mean considerable sacrifice—in time, if not money. In other centuries, only the richest pilgrims traveled by coach or horseback; the rest went on foot. But rich or poor, the time which such an undertaking would require was indeed significant.

And it *was* an act of faith. There was no assurance that the pilgrimage would bring one closer to God. One could only hope.

Meanwhile, the enemy was constantly whispering, for his best chance of dissuading the pilgrim was in that time leading up to the determination to go. Nothing will change, he murmured. Your heart will come home as barren as it is now, and your purse will be as empty as your soul. Your work will be taken over by another, and those who now mock you behind your back, will laugh openly and call you a fool.

Yet there was another voice—still and small, appealing to the heart of the pilgrim: Come. Leave the distraction and despair behind. Separate yourself unto me. And fear not, for I will go with you. Come.

If the pilgrim heeded his spirit, as it yearned for the Spirit of God, if he gave not in to the reasoning of his intellect or the willfulness of his soul which did not want to make the sacrifices or endure the hardships, then eventually the time to depart would come. Leading up to that moment, the arguments against going would continue to rise and swell to a crescendo.

But once he actually set forth, a sense of peace would settle over him. Grace would surround him. God honors even the smallest steps of obedience.

The enemy, however, was far from finished; he may have lost the first battle, but there would be many more contests before the outcome of the campaign was decided. At the moment, he was regrouping, but it would not be long before he counter-attacked—more subtly this time.

A short distance into the journey, where the way grew difficult, the pilgrim gave in to the temptation to look back: should he have come? When so much was hanging in the balance at home? What had he been thinking of? With that door open, suddenly he was assailed by doubts: it was cruel, selfish, heartless of you to leave your wife and little one in such need. How can they manage without you? It was irresponsible to leave at seed-time ... especially when your neighbor covets your field ... even now he is probably talking to the landlord about you....

Now the pilgrim was vulnerable; the pilgrimage itself was in jeopardy. He could be turned. You can be home very quickly, the hard voice murmured. You can tell them that you came to your senses and realized what a foolish thing it was that you were doing. They would accept that; nothing would be lost. You merely suffered a momentary lapse of sanity, that was all. But you must return *now*.

The other voice was also there; very still, very small—so small that the pilgrim could hear it only by stopping and praying. And listening. Remember why you came, it said.

Remember what you once had. The serenity of resting in the hollow of God's hand. The bliss of being raised up to meet His gaze. The eternity of knowing His delight in you. Remember why you came.

The pilgrim heard—and remembered. And resumed his journey.

The next test came in the form of a stranger, who sought to distract him from his purpose and perhaps lure him into sin. It had been a long journey and would be longer still—what harm could there be in tarrying awhile? In partaking in some refreshment and worldly discourse, which was really no different than what others did all the time. No different than what the pilgrim himself had done often enough at home.

If he prayed then, he might hear the small voice saying: but you are not home now. And while you are in the world, while you are on this pilgrimage, you are not of the world. If you are weary, and feel in need of refreshment, slake your thirst at the well of Living Water. There your spirit will be refreshed and renewed, the appetites of your flesh will be subdued, and your soul will know peace.

The pilgrim did pray and was refreshed and journeyed on. Alone. And that was the next test. For in all his life, he had never felt so alone. There might be others on the path with him; indeed, he might find himself surrounded by friends.

But he was still alone. So alone that he longed for his wife, his children, his mother. Those who loved him. How he longed to spend just a moment with someone who cared.

But he was *not* alone. That was another ploy of the enemy, whose tricks were growing ever more subtle. For in truth the Lord God who had assigned him this journey, was with him. Always. Every step of the way. All he had to do was stop and pray. (From a distance, as a pilgrim, he could see his loved ones with greater clarity and completeness—and embrace them as never before.)

So he did. And he was reminded of what the First Pilgrim had given up, to make His pilgrimage. Matthew had recorded His words: *Foxes have dens, and the birds of the sky have nests, but the Son of Man has nowhere to rest his head.* Jesus' life was a pilgrimage. To go on it, He had given up everything. And in the end, He would give up His life, too.

The pilgrims saw, then, that it was necessary to give up the comforts of home and family and loved ones, to be completely free to know God. And as his pilgrimage continued, bit by bit he was drawing closer to God.

He had picked up his old habit of praying with the heart—it was like an idle tool which had grown rusty from lack of use. But it still worked. It still fit the hand. And with use, the rust began to wear off.

He was also learning to listen with the heart. And to see with the heart. As he traveled, his spirit was awakening. Gradually he was coming to perceive that his journey was a quest—a spiritual adventure, undertaken at God's behest. On it, nothing happened by accident. There were no chance meetings, no coincidental remarks. Some things which befell him might not be aligned with the center of God's perfect will for him; some might be fiery darts from the enemy. But even those, he came to see, were within the bounds of God's permissive will. For the enemy could not afflict him without God allowing it.

Therefore, in everything that happened to him there was either a lesson, a reward, or a test. God was waiting to see how he would respond: would he heed his flesh, his soul, or his spirit?

And now, in His infinite mercy, God gave him a fellow pilgrim for companionship along the way.

He was joined by someone else who was going to the same holy place at the same time, with the same hopes and expectations. Someone else was learning similar lessons and facing similar tests. He had never been alone in spirit; now he was no longer alone in the flesh.

To pass the time, the two pilgrims told each other their stories, ending with how they came to be on this pilgrimage. In the process, each took the measure of the other's heart. When the pilgrims decided that they could trust one another, they now shared not only feelings, but dreams and aspirations.

As they did, a bond began to form between them. It was a bond forged in the fire of shared adversity, and tempered in the water, the water of shared prayer. It was a bond that would last long after the pilgrimage was over, and the pilgrims parted ways. They discovered each other, like many do, coming from the East and from the West. In pilgrimage they discovered the world in and around themselves.

Like a long river approaching its mouth, the way of the pilgrims was broadening now, fed by other tributaries from other villages, other lands. There were many pilgrims walking with them now, and behind and ahead of them, speaking in foreign tongues, as well as recognizable dialects. In spirit, it was a gathering, not a crowd, for all had a common purpose and a common call. And there was an undercurrent of joy and anticipation, for their destination was close at hand.

When at last he arrived, our pilgrim's heart was full. So strong were his emotions, he could not trust himself to speak. He wanted to pray in a quiet place, but the holy site was thronged with pilgrims. Then he found one. He knelt and thanked God for bringing him, and for all that He had shown him. For he realized that that had been part of His plan; as he had journeyed, God had begun a work in him. He prayed that it would be a work that would never stop.

When he arose, he felt great peace. In the ensuing holy days, he joined in the processions, the worship, the singing and solemn assemblies, and the traditional rituals of that place. In each, he was able to keep his heart and mind and soul and being centered on God, and only Him. And each act, each inner revelation, was etched indelibly on the bronze tablet of his memory. Over the years the edges might weather, but they would never be forgotten.

Before each pilgrim left, God would confront him (or her) with the ultimate challenge: *Make your life a pilgrimage. On the journey now completed, you have begun to see things as I see them. Keep this. Treasure it. For this, not the world, is reality. This is eternity. I want you to share this with me, always. And so I will go with you always, even unto the ends of the earth. Will you go that far with me?*

If the pilgrim's heart said yes, his life would be forever altered. He already knew that he was a different person than he had been when he left home. Now, in spirit, he would never be that person again. There was no remorse, no looking back. There was only peace and great joy.

For some pilgrims, this point is indeed accompanied by signs and wonders. But for most it will be a quiet, growing contentment that will stay with them even in the midst of the most trying circumstances, as they continue on their eternal pilgrimage.

# 11

# A Pilgrim Today

A pilgrimage is a living prayer, containing all dimensions of human activity—physical, spiritual, and emotional. What motivates a modern man to make a pilgrimage? Often it is a sense of life being a dead end, or that the world has become totally absurd, or that he is simply "sick and tired of everything." Sometimes this is combined with an awareness that God is calling him in a new direction, and that he desires to create a new communication between himself and God.

And sometimes a man does not know God, but is aware of his own inner, original need for Him—he has, in fact, been constantly searching for the One who is both near and unknown. And though physical illness or just curiosity appears to provide the initial spark, this search may be the real reason such a man decides to go on pilgrimage.

Once the decision is made, each step becomes important, for the spiritual process of pilgrimage includes—and requires—experiences that touch unknown and unhealed areas inside our personality. Perhaps the most dramatic step, other than the actual leaving, comes when the pilgrim must pay for the trip.

In ancient times, the cost of a pilgrimage was reckoned more in time than in money. Today, it is the opposite. In the age of the jet airplane, even a mountain village as remote as Medjugorje can be reached in a day or two. But while travel by jet saves a great deal of time, it takes a great deal of money. Often people use their last savings or even borrow the money to come. For most, the financial sacrifice becomes part of the living prayer that is pilgrimage.

Where once a pilgrimage to a distant holy place took weeks, or even months, today the transition is almost instant. And so, one of the great blessings of pilgrimage has been lost: there is no time for change to occur within the pilgrim traveling to a holy place.

Today, many people arrive in Medjugorje physically, while their minds and emotions are still back home. They worry about the lack of news of the outside world, of a reliable phone system with which to call home, of comforts they have come to regard as necessities. If it is winter, the tile floors of the homes in which they are quartered are shockingly cold to their bare feet in the middle of the night. They do not know that in Hercegovina, heat is a luxury.

The food is strange to them. The bread is coarse, the vegetables do not resemble those in American supermarkets, the meat is greasy. The cheese is strong, the coffee is bitter, the spices are unfamiliar. If one is looking for things to be unhappy about, he has not far to look.

Once, when the journey took days or weeks, the pilgrim arrived at the holy place with only gratitude in his heart. Today, the gratitude comes, but it takes time. People arrive exhausted, physically and emotionally. No one sleeps well on a plane, especially when it is bearing him as a stranger to a strange land. Also, it is likely that with the added pain of troubling farewells, one's last night at home was none too restful. Many pilgrims arrive here having had little or no sleep for two or even three days. Anyone who has done that, knows what state their emotions are in.

Some people have demanded a change in accommodations. To something more familiar, possibly one of the new Communist hotels, with private bathrooms and ample hot water. Their tour leaders go to great trouble to make these changes, and perhaps after two or three days, they are able to produce them.

But in that time, the pilgrims have become grateful. "Oh, please, don't make us move," they say. "Let us stay with our families! We have grown to love them!"

But what of the lack of heat? The need for a private bath?

"Well—we were wrong. We don't mind anymore. After all, are we not on a pilgrimage?"

Happily they have come to realize it in a remarkably short time. While the world has been much compressed by modern travel, the process of pilgrimage remains the same. Gradually, in the pilgrim's mind and heart, the things of God replace the things of the world.

In Medjugorje, that process is speeded up by the fasting that all pilgrims do.

"But we are not fasting," they might say. "In fact, we are probably eating too much."

Nonetheless, they *are* fasting—and in a manner prescribed by the Blessed Mother in her messages. For they are fasting from the cares and distractions of the world. And the fast is achieving the intended result of all fasts: it is intensifying their relationship with God.

Consider for a moment: there is no television or radio, no telephones or fax machines, no newspapers or magazines. Instead, there is silence—and this is the great freedom of pilgrimage. It is a different environment, unimposing but nonetheless felt deeply. In that silence the pilgrim can hear God. And for the duration of his stay here, God will have his undivided attention.

How often in his life has that happened?

As gratitude grows in the heart of the pilgrim, so does the impulse to give. In the eyes of the world, the giving of pilgrims is irrational and naive, and the world laughs at them. But giving is a necessary and important part of the complete picture of a spiritual pilgrimage. It is a prayer of its own kind. Giving and receiving is natural to a pilgrimage, and is part of its goal. It should be natural to the Christian life.

Recently a collection was made in Medjugorje for the Church in Albania. As the basket was extended, I felt it was the hand of God. And He was asking us to put not only money, but ourselves, into that basket. A part of the Body of Christ needed us.

When money is freely given, and used in a Mother Theresa type of way, it does become a prayer—the fruit of Christian charity, bringing life where life is needed. When we give our material possessions and our time, we create a condition in the world where God's work is felt in a true way. Every prayer is an act of giving—and prayer may not be proven true, unless it includes giving.

For a pilgrim, then, money should flow freely, like an unobstructed stream. He should give freely, and be given to freely. Many pilgrims are stunned by the spontaneous generosity of the people of Medjugorje—not so much with money, of which they have very little, but with their food, their homes, their lives. Little acts of kindness—which are not so little.

This is not accidental. Our Lady has called the people who live here to express the hospitality and love of her Son to the pilgrims. They are to be "a sea of holiness." She has instructed the people of Medjugorje to regard money as a way of prayer and a tool of prayer. Through it, the Church accomplishes her mission. In their dealings with pilgrims they are to avoid emphasis on the transactional aspects of the business of providing transportation, food, lodging, and religious articles. As our Lord tells us: His work will be recognized by its fruits.

Sometimes a misunderstanding can occur. When a person on a pilgrimage is touched by the Holy Spirit and becomes completely available for God's work, he also becomes vulnerable. The one who is serving the pilgrims is also a pilgrim, in a sense, and should receive as a pilgrim, immediately seeking a way to give. The giving and receiving should be like love, which is always seeking new ways to prove itself.

But as the flow of pilgrims has increased, so has the temptation of those serving them, to regard money as the ultimate goal of their work. When this happens, the Church suffers tremendously. It is more than sinning against the spirit of what God is doing; it is stealing from the Holy Spirit. And Jesus called sinning against the Holy Spirit, the most serious sin of all. Travel agencies, local people receiving pilgrims, guides—and priests—must take great care not to commit this sin. Serving the pilgrims is a special work of the Church, one that requires true spiritual honesty and discipline.

The priests, like all the others who are serving the pilgrims, are like a river canyon: the spiritual and material graces and gifts of God should come and flow through them. Their first responsibility is to distribute the graces of God—those spiritual in the Sacraments, and those material in physical buildings, or to feed the poor.

In a true Church, everyone is a pilgrim, and everyone is giving. And when a pilgrim gives, a worldly obstacle is removed—enabling God to come and give Himself.

Once in California I was given a rosary. A lady had made it herself, and she gave it without a word. The gift would speak for her.

It did. To me, it was like love: love is not jealous, it is not inflated, it is not rude, it does not seek its own interests. Such a gift bears love and prayer, and it requires love and prayer. It is a gift that brings blessing upon both the giver and the receiver.

I am a Franciscan; my pockets are as empty as any pilgrim's. But my soul is filled with the love of so many who have given like the poor widow. Beginning with the love of my mother, who gave everything that a mother could give to her children.

There is a mystery to divinely inspired giving. Those who give never come at a wrong time, but are always sent by God. When we were building a mission church in Konjic, we had laid the foundation—and run out of money. A lady from Madrid, not known to us, came and said, "I would like to help." The church was completed. Our Lady, Queen of Peace, for whom the church was named, had this woman in her plan. She would not allow the church to be left unfinished. Each one who has helped is like a bead on the rosary of God's goodness in the world. And each one is a mystery—one station in the life of Jesus in our midst.

The main blessing of pilgrimage will always be the extra grace on each pilgrim which enables him to put God first. That is what conversion means. And conversion is the heart of the message of Medjugorje.

That grace is a precious gift, not to be wasted. The pilgrim should take advantage of it, every moment. Praying and fasting. Asking God to suggest penances—acts of thoughtfulness or selflessness, where formerly one might have behaved selfishly. There is grace for confession. And if the pilgrim feels the need of that Sacrament, he should do it today, not tomorrow. There is grace for repentance. If he asks God to show him where He would have him change, God will answer. He always does. There is grace for forgiveness, and for the first steps of reconciliation.

And there is grace for conversion—for beginning the pilgrimage of life. It is an ongoing, inner pilgrimage which people of deep spirituality can achieve without going to a specific, physical destination. It is an attitude of the mind and of the heart.

Our Lord said: *I am the Way, the Truth, and the Life.* The pilgrim knows He is the Way and the Truth. Now he must learn that He is the Life.

# 12

# Commitment

Commitment—the word comes up often in Medjugorje. Commitment to a marriage, to a family, to a job, a vocation, a relationship. It means that once you give your word, you keep it. A commitment should make the future as unalterable as the past. The tragedy of our time is that people are questioning their commitments.

Today, the world prefers everything to be relative— relative values, relative ethics. It shuns absolutes and considers it not such a bad thing to break a promise....

God does not see it that way, so be very careful what you promise Him. He will expect you to keep your word.

One promise which is constantly tested is our commitment to our faith. In Hercegovina, the Communists made that commitment very costly. If you remained a Christian, there would be no good job for you, no promotion, no career. The only thing you could count on was continual harassment. And there could be prison.

But the government was not able to crush the faith. Instead, there was a purification there. If you wanted to keep your faith, you paid a very dear price for it. There are many people in Hercegovina who have suffered for their commitment to God, and who have redeemed their faith.

In my country the faith was challenged but not destroyed. In America, the challenge to the faith is different, and I don't know in which place the faith has been hurt more. History will tell us. It has already recorded the collapse of the Communist system. But I am not sure that the Capitalist system will stand the test of time. The West has so many interdependent life-support systems, like an elaborate spider's web. Energy, banking, communications—if one of these were to suddenly fail, would it bring the others down? The collapse of the West might be even more dramatic than the collapse of the East.

The only values that will last will be the values of faith. To these alone should we remain committed.

Another commitment we must take very seriously is our commitment to the future. Are we called to marry? Is that God's intention for our life? If so, then do not later wonder: was it a mistake?

The only mistake is in asking that question! Some things cannot be questioned.

Are you called to become a priest? Then once that commitment is made, the future is done. Our future is like homework which needs to be finished.

The most tragic lack of commitment today, is to new life. Once human life has begun, can it be undone? That is like looking at your children and saying: can this one be unborn? That one? To think that way is tragic ignorance of reality—which is present there in its past form and future form, like the future tree which is contained in the seed.

Abortion is a tragic attack on the future. For when that commitment to the future is destroyed, all other existing and future commitments, if not ruined, are terribly wounded.

When people ask me questions about personal commitments, I remind them of what happened at the wedding feast in Cana of Galilee. In the midst of the celebration, there was a crisis: the wine ran out. Well, in each person's life, there comes a moment when there is no wine. The shape or extent of the crisis does not matter; there will come a time when we run out of wine.

What does matter is what we do then. If we are wise, and if we have invited appropriate guests to our celebration of life, we will go to the Master of the Feast and inform Him.

Or if we go first to His mother, she will point us to Him, just as she did the wine stewards, saying, "Do what He tells you."

The point to remember is: the old wine must go away—for the new wine to come. And in between, when there is no wine, we must be patient. And we must trust God. He will never allow us to drink old wine which has gone sour. He always wants to improve the quality of the wine. For those who are patient, the new wine will be much better than the old!

The mistake many make is their methodology. They think: the wine is gone, so the way to get wine back is to undo the past and to begin a new future. But God wants us to continue into the future which we have already begun. He wants us to build on the foundation which He has already given us. If we will do that, the new wine will come.

What a mistake it would be for me to leave the priesthood, just because the wine appears to have run out! What a mistake it would be for you to leave your marriage, the moment the wine jars are empty! What a mistake to start another foundation of marriage, in an attempt to bring back happiness!

Sometimes, God likes me to be out of wine. I plead with Him then, as His mother had directed us, and I pray for the grace to be patient. In time, the new wine will come. A new building will be built on the original foundation. And the new wine will be better!

Some people say: you know, what I committed myself to was a mistake. I will undo it; I will begin something completely new. But what they are really saying is: God Himself has made a mistake.

That is a stupid thing to say—and it has tragic consequences.

I have a friend who has had some very difficult moments in his marriage. He told me that only their children enabled him to stay on. But he did stay. It took a while for the new wine to come. But now they are happy again together; in fact, they have a better marriage than ever before.

It may take a while—quite a while—but be patient and of good courage; the new wine will come.

# 13

# Vocations

Leo XIII, speaking prophetically at the end of his pontificate, declared that the final century of this millennium would belong to Satan. In it, the Evil One would launch a full-scale assault on the Church, on the faith, and on all members of the Body of Christ.

It is not our purpose to assess the theological strength of this teaching. But one cannot help noting the world-wide spread of Communism, Masonry, New Age, and other anti-Christian (and anti-human) beliefs, to say nothing of pornography, abortion, and drug abuse that we are now experiencing.

The enemy is familiar with the Book of Revelation. He knows the fate that awaits him, and he knows his time is almost at an end. Filled with hate, and furious that he is powerless to delay the outcome, he is attacking on all fronts simultaneously. The more souls he can harvest, the more grief he can cause in the heart of God.

It is no surprise, then, that the religious vocations are among his chief targets. This is understandable:

throughout history, the living examples of nuns and monks and priests have given witness to all mankind that it is possible to surrender all for Christ. As long as men and women accepted God's call to lives of sacrifice and obedience, they would represent the ultimate alternative to what the world had to offer. Anyone profoundly moved by the eternal love of God, who wanted to give all back to Him, would have that option.

In some lands, where the faith is still strong, or where it has recently been strongly renewed, there is no shortage of candidates for religious orders. But in other lands, where the faith was traditionally strong for centuries, but now has been seriously weakened, there is a crisis. In many convents and monasteries, the average age is now over 60. Such is the shortage of priests that many seminary preparatory schools have closed, and the average age of the priesthood is climbing rapidly.

Why?

In our time, the call of faith—to put God's will first—is seen as totally opposed to contemporary secular thinking. Satan's propaganda is subtle and, to modern ears, seductive: Why on earth would you want to become a priest? You have so many talents, such a future ahead of you—why throw it all away? Your family has such hopes for you! They want you to succeed, to marry, to raise your own family one day. They will never understand!

And that is the saddest part: for many families are no longer centered on God, as they once were. In a family where the faith is still strong, a religious vocation is not only respected; it is admired. A family feels honored, blessed, when God calls one of their number to His special service.

But the modern Western world, with all its choices and diversions, with its subliminal endorsement of youthful rebellion, has weakened the family unit. It is much more difficult for parents there to create and maintain a holy environment in their homes, in which to raise their children.

As a result, the children have come to question not only their parents' authority, but their traditions, their faith—everything. And as they themselves become adults, it is they and not their parents who represent society. Gradually the attitude of society changes. No longer are priests and sisters held in high regard. Now they are tolerated, and in some places, scorned.

One is tempted to wonder how long such societies would survive without them. In the Old Testament, certain wicked cities were spared because of the presence of a handful of devout believers.... And even if God's Day of Judgment is not as close at hand as some believe, if you remove the Church and the faith, you remove the last restraint on wanton selfishness. You will see people turn on one another, rend themselves to pieces.

The problem today is that society has put such a premium on success and power and prestige that the importance of the role of the priest and the nun has been forgotten. Yet those with religious vocations are most intimately and existentially necessary, for they are to society what the immune system is to the human body. As the vocations grow fewer, the immune system becomes progressively weaker—until it can no longer withstand the evil that seeks to invade the body. Then the immune system collapses, and the body falls prey to the next virus that attacks it.

But society, instead of being grateful for each priest and nun, as in all previous centuries, resents them. Their mere presence confronts the conscience. The religious does not have to say a word; the habit or the collar speaks volumes. It says that there is another way. It says that perhaps the values that modern society has invested so heavily in are bankrupt.

Society does not much care for the reminder. There is, in fact, a hardened element in society that not only resents being reminded, but responds with something approaching delight whenever a priest or nun falls. Where once there might have been sorrow or compassion—and a period of anonymous grace during which the sinner might be granted an opportunity to repent, and eventually be restored to some useful service—now there is no mercy shown. Forgotten is the example of Jesus, who said, "Your sins are forgiven. Go, and sin no more." Instead, the hardened element in society heeds a harsher voice: He held himself to be holier than the rest of us, didn't he? Well, the hypocrite deserves eternal disgrace! They're all hypocrites!

And by so declaring, that element hopes to lessen the discomfort at the sight of the next habit or collar.

Priests and nuns, even those who may one day be canonized, are far from perfect, as they themselves will readily attest. But their very imperfections make them, in a way, the more poignant reminders, as they struggle to live up to the promises they made to God.

There was, of course, one perfect reminder, who came not for the righteous, but for sinners. He forgave the fallen, encouraged those whose resolve was failing, strengthened the faint at heart. And one recalls how much the Pharisees appreciated being reminded that as spiritual leaders, they were expected to show people by their own example the way to true holiness. In the end, the Pharisees either had to repent—or destroy the reminder.

Today, with the flow of young hearts responding to religious vocations having slowed almost to a trickle, the enemy is now directing an all-out attack on those already in the priesthood. If the modern mentality of some affluent societies regards becoming a priest stupid, it regards anyone remaining a priest as pathetic. In many ways, priests in such societies are under more difficult persecution than was suffered by the priests of Hercegovina under Communism.

At least here the evil was exposed and clearly defined, and the majority of the people were with them. But in some western societies, the attitude towards the priesthood has deteriorated to the point where a priest needs all the faith he can summon, just to remain in his call.

The social isolation of many priests today creates great loneliness—and great danger. How will he fill his non-working hours? Will the temptations of the modern world eat away at time which was once spent in prayer and reflection? Will he succumb to watching mindless television? To alcohol? To letting his mind wander where it shouldn't? To relationships that are wrong and ultimately devastating?

Traditionally, nuns have looked after priests in rectories and monasteries, providing the balance of a woman's presence. They were like sisters in the sense of a sacred family, sharing a life of consecrated devotion with their priest brothers. The rectory was more than a place where one worked; it was a home, and when priests and nuns shared prayer, it was a redeeming family, supporting one another with the same commitment and the same vision of life.

Now there are so few nuns in some Western societies that the Church's equivalent of family life is, in many parishes, no longer possible. For lay women cannot take the place of nuns, any more than a layman can take the place of a priest. But the absence of nuns leaves a solitary priest's life even lonelier—and more vulnerable.

The same is true for nuns. They need the fellowship of priests within the Church family, just as the priests need them. But sadly, many sisters in the West are as socially isolated today as priests—and as lonely. And vulnerable. Modern society encourages sisters and priests to go their own way apart from one another, searching and asking for new roads, new independences.

When unhealthy relationships do occur between priests and nuns, in the way of competitions, accusations, lack of trust, striving for independence and emancipation, it is precisely because the family aspect has been missing from their lives for so long.

The lack of encouragement of, and support for, the traditional ways can be traced back to early childhood—which says again that the foundation for a healthy society is a healthy family. Strong families produce strong priests and strong sisters. But sadly, what can be found in many rectories today is a mirror of what can be found in many lay families: solo television-watching (if others are similarly absorbed, one might as well be alone) has replaced shared meals and conversation, and communal prayer.

If the enemy, in his assault on the priesthood, cannot lure a priest into destructive, exploitable sin, then he will do all he can to persuade him to forsake his vows. Father, you are about to celebrate your fiftieth birthday—who cares? If your mother were alive, she would remember, and send you a cake. But even if you had a cake now, who would you blow out the candles with? You have given the Church the best years of your life and what have you gotten in return? Nothing but the certainty that you will be as alone for the remaining years until retirement, as you are right now.

And then what? An old priests' home?

On the other hand, if you were to give that woman the slightest reason to hope, she could make a nice home for you, share the evenings with you, and be there to grow old with....

And if the enemy cannot persuade a priest to leave, then he will do his utmost to discourage him, dropping thoughts and grievances into the pool of his self-pity until it becomes a swamp of despair, and into his despair until it becomes apathy. Then the priest will be completely neutralized. Where once the Spirit of Christ blazed within him, fanning the embers of those around him until they too burst into flame, now that spirit is but a dim and fading memory, like the last tinge of color on the western horizon, long after the sun has set.

I am not advocating marriage for Catholic priests. The call to the priesthood has never changed—and it never will. Just as the call to become a sister has never changed.

What *has* changed is society's attitude towards such a call. It is now so negative that I sense that many young people, deeply inspired by the Spirit of God, nonetheless automatically discount the possibility of serving Him as a religious. God would never ask me to do such a thing! I will teach for Him, become a doctor for Him, raise a fine family for Him—I am ready to serve Him anywhere, anytime. But He would never want me to do that.

Oh? Have you asked Him?

For many, the vocation of priest lacks glamour, adventure. But that is the world's view. Compare it to the vocation of a military pilot. The priest soars, too, but inward. He, too, faces mortal combat, but when he is hit, there is Someone to repair his machine and ready him for another flight. If the pilot lives to grow old, he no longer flies. But the longer a priest lives, the more daring his flights become. And there is always a fight to be fought, and a peace to be won.

The moment you ask God if He is calling you to a religious vocation, the enemy will fill your mind with all the delights of the world that you would have to give up. To relinquish the right to own, to choose, and to marry—no one in their right mind would do that!

And what if the superior in your convent or monastery or diocese turns out to be insensitive or perhaps unintentionally cruel; you will have no redress.

It *is* true that you will have to trust God with your life and future. But you have the word of the testimony of thousands upon thousands of religious throughout the ages that not only can you trust Him, but you will find challenge and fulfillment beyond anything you could have imagined. There will be times of great difficulty, but they will be balanced by times of great joy. Above all, you will find the peace—His peace—which truly does pass all understanding.

Unfortunately, the opposite is also true: if God is calling you to become a religious, then your heart and spirit will never be content anywhere else. You may achieve all the success the world has to offer; you may be the envy of all who know you. But you will not have peace, and you will know there was another way…

Too late, you realize why. You can ask God to forgive you, and He will. You can surrender the rest of your life to Him, to use as He desires, and He will. But you cannot take back and live over the life behind you—that perhaps was meant to have been lived in holy orders.

So—if you suspect that God might be calling you to become a priest or a sister, do not hastily discard that notion. Listen in your heart for His voice; if you are willing to hear Him, then you will hear Him. And if the self-will of your soul is strong, you may have to pray, "Lord, make me willing to be willing…." Listen for the still, small voice that you have come to love. The courageous will act.

It will be all too easy to hear the enemy at such a time. When he is alarmed, he tends to over-react— and nothing alarms him more than a young heart contemplating a vocation! The world, your parents, your friends may be shocked and may attempt to persuade you out of it. They will mean well, but they will not be speaking for God.

Go inward. Get to a quiet place and spend time alone with God in the chambers of your heart. Read the stories of the great heroes of the faith. See how they received their vocations. Do not be dismayed if this answer does not come as readily as some others. In a decision as momentous as this, God is not going to make up your mind for you. You must reach for Him, even as He is reaching for you.

When your hands clasp, it is done.

# 14

# A Holy Environment

When God created man, He also created the perfect environment in which to place him: the Garden of Eden. It was a place of beauty, harmony, and peace — a holy place, where God delighted to walk with man in the cool of the day. Man was busy during the rest of the day, for God had given him much to do, tending the Garden and naming all the plants and animals in it.

When God created a woman for him, man's happiness was complete.

But because God had made man as a companion, to share time and eternity with Him, He gave man free will. (There is little satisfaction in sharing with a creature who cannot think for itself, who always does and says exactly what you intend it to.) He loved His creation, and He wanted man to choose to do His will, out of love for Him. But man had to able to freely choose.

And so, there had to be the possibility of man's making the wrong choice. For if there were only good things to choose from, where would man's love for his Father be tested? So into that holy environment, God allowed the winged serpent to enter. And He allowed the serpent to tempt His creations to disobey the only rule that He had given them.

The man and woman believed the lie of the serpent: that their Father had lied to them, and that the consequences would not be as severe as He had clearly warned them. They made the wrong choice—and discovered too late that God had been telling the truth. They were banished forever from the Garden, to wander and toil as lost souls in the wilderness.

But God still loved his children, still hoped that they would turn back to Him. Whenever they took the slightest step in His direction, He would bless them. And there was always sufficient grace available to them, to choose His ways over their own. Each step of obedience He would honor, and whenever His children did turn to Him and ask from the heart for Him to help them, He did.

Often, however, after He preserved them or prospered them, they would lose sight of Him, and begin to think that they had done it themselves. They would turn from Him and live for themselves—and eventually succumb to jealousy and pride and envy and hatred. They began to treat one another abusively, and even make war on one another.

God would wait—until some of those who once knew Him would become so miserable that they would look up and seek His face and turn from their wicked ways. Then He would heed their prayers and heal their land. And for a generation or two, or perhaps more, they would remain grateful, striving to do His will.

He would be pleased and would bless them more — and gradually they would forget.

In ancient days, He would remind them before it was too late. He would send prophets to speak for Him, to convict the hearts of those who could still be reached. Some would hear, and repent. But others would stone his prophets and kill them. Finally He gave His only begotten Son. Many did hear Him then, and the faith began to spread. But in the end, they killed Him, too.

The serpent had only bruised His heel, however; the faith was established and continued to grow. Many, able to freely choose between good and evil, chose the good. More than once, the Spirit of God swept the known world, each time extending the borders of Christendom further, until they reached to the ends of the earth.

At other times, especially in this century, evil appeared to be invincible. People who did not know God would ask: if God is good, how can He permit a Hitler? A Stalin? The answer is simple: God made the rules. He gave man free will. If men freely choose to follow an agent of the evil one, God is not going to remove their freedom of choice. If He were to break His rules now, the game would be over. It must be played to the end.

But note something: those evils which had once loomed so ominously were vanquished.

Why?

Because enough good men and women prayed.

Just as we forget God, we forget the power of prayer. The Blessed Mother has reminded us that prayer can even stop wars! Hard to believe? Ten years ago, she began asking Medjugorje pilgrims (and anyone else who would listen), to pray for peace. Enough men and women took her at her word and prayed, believing. To the dumbfoundment of the entire world, Communism, in the twinkling of an eye, collapsed. Do you think anything but prayer did that?

Until the last generation or so, given a choice between good and evil, more often than not men and women chose good. But in a powerful way in our time the evil one has been laying the foundation of an unholy environment that would change that. In places of higher learning he has flattered the intellect for three generations, so that today's teachers are impressing on young minds what they themselves had been taught: man does not need God. With the power of his intellect he can solve his problems and make the world a better place to live in.

In the Body of Christ, he sowed discord and division, knowing that a house divided against itself could not stand. In society he encouraged young idealists to believe in the nobility of man alone. Did the Bible teach that because of the original sin of the first man and woman, man was a fallen creature? That was a myth! The Bible was a collection of fairy tales, perpetrated by those who wanted to hold others in condemnation. Man was inherently good!

Many men chose to believe the serpent's lie. A generation of scientists arose, saying: "Bring us your problems; with our modern technology we will solve them." Only for every problem they solved, they seemed to create ten others that no one had foreseen. They created a fertilizer to promote faster growth—and wound up poisoning the very plants they meant to help, as well as the ground and the water around them. They invented new ways to convert oxygen to carbon dioxide, but could not reverse the process. Only a tree leaf could do that—and they did not know how.

And when all this was pointed out to them, they said: "Well, we are not God, are we?"

No, they are not. Though many have regarded them as such.

The idealists and social engineers have said much the same: Bring us your poor, your disaffected and disenfranchised. With our modem geopolitical and psychological understanding, we will solve the world's problems.

But they are not God, either.

Yet man continues to prefer his own solutions to God's. The teachers continue to urge young minds to believe only in themselves. The world continues to hold up success as the only goal worth achieving, while the faith continues to weaken—to the degree that pornography is blatant and rampant. It is now everywhere—not just in print but in clothes and speech and entertainment and lifestyles. You cannot go out without being assaulted by it. And if you complain, idealists remind you of the individual's right to freely choose. If you wonder what happened to society's right to freely choose, you will find that in three generations the enemy has so worn down society's will to resist and dulled its senses that it scarcely sees or hears what once would have caused outrage. And if that is pointed out, society shrugs: what can we do? It's hopeless.

If pornography has blunted society's awareness, abortion—murder for the sake of convenience—has so calloused society's heart that life does not have a tenth the value it once had. And we are not talking merely about agnostics; that includes many people who claim to believe in God. (Society does not like to bring God into the issue of abortion. No one wants to think about how God must feel about millions of new lives, each of which He allowed to begin, being wantonly snuffed out.)

When new life is so devalued, so is old life. Where once a family cared for its oldest members, now they are put into nursing homes. For some families, where there are no available care-givers and no funds, there is no choice. But too often it is done for the sake of convenience.

When new life and old life are no longer of value, young life comes next. When I was a little child, my mother was there, when I needed her. Today, many children are deprived, continually, of the presence of their mothers. In broken homes, the mothers have no choice; they must support their families. But in too many modern homes, they are earning second incomes, to obtain more of the material things that the world has to offer. Or to pursue careers— rejecting the God-given call to motherhood.

Their children suffer. Through no choice of their own, they must endure loneliness and indifferent treatment in day-care centers or at the hands of hired baby-sitters. At moments of emotional crisis they will never know a mother's tender love. And by its absence they may be scarred for the rest of their lives.

Any working mother who is not forced to work by circumstances, should ask God: does He want her to continue? Or does He want her to return to her home and be a spiritual stronghold for her family? (The husband may be the head of the family, but so often the woman is its heart.) If she is in such conflict over it that she cannot hear Him, let her ask herself this: would the heavenly Father have entrusted her child or children into the care of her and her husband, had it been known that the children would not have the presence of a mother?

Hearts that have become indifferent to new life, old life, and young life, can also become brutal: where once physical violence within the family was almost unheard of, now it is becoming commonplace.

The evil one's unholy environment is now complete and in place.

A child's first environment is the womb, where hopefully he knows nothing but love. His next environment is the nursery, watched over by a loving mother. Then it is the home, where both parents are responsible for the environment. After that, there is school—and even parochial schools no longer provide the environment they once did. Between school and home is the environment of the streets, the neighborhood—an environment on which parents and Church have less and less influence. A husband and wife, soon to be parents, should pick their neighborhood environment with care—if they can. Many can't, and often little can be done to improve neighborhood environments. The creative hand of God could do wonders with such an environment—but the evil one uses every modern tool in the world to stop the hand of God. In the streets today, all too often it is the devil who calls the tune.

Nor is he confined to the streets. The world's unholiness now seeps into the home environment in so many ways—through television and radio, magazines, clothing, even advertising. It hangs in the very air. The modern world's environment represents the collective choices, values, customs and traditions of society—and everything fits into it. Thus, a child—surrounded, influenced and ultimately molded by that environment from the day he was born—never has to choose evil; the choice has been made for him, long ago.

Millions of young hearts that in earlier times, in a holy environment, might have heard the call of God, will not. Without any conscious decision for evil, they will grow in the direction of evil, and with very little effort on his part, the enemy will harvest them like ripe fruit falling from a tree.

There is an antidote.

God still loves His children. He has sent one more prophet: the one who first introduced His Son to the world, has returned to re-introduce the world to His Son. From the moment that Jesus, from the Cross, gave John to her as her son, Mary has loved all men and women as if they were her own. Now she is calling them—to conversion if they do not know God, and repentance if they do. Nineteen million pilgrims have come to the place where she is appearing, and many have gone home determined to live the messages that she has been giving. Around the world, millions more, without having been to Medjugorje, are doing the same.

And the result? Holy environments are being created, to offset the one so powerfully entrenched in the modern world. A holy environment begins in the heart.

A heart, open to God, becomes a place of devotion. The sweet scent of prayer fills that place like incense — and drives the devil from it, for he can not stand that fragrance. Which is why it is so important to pray much, from the heart and in the heart. And why the Blessed Mother has urged us to pray the rosary — familiar prayers, prayed often enough, become internalized; we pray without being aware of it.

When the heart has become a holy environment, the blood that it pumps through the body cleanses and purifies the members. Health is restored and even an affliction that remains, no longer is a source of bitterness or despair. Such a heart can now reach out to others. Acutely sensitive to the burdens of another heart, it can help carry that burden. It can help many burdened hearts.

Holiness radiates from such a heart and begins to create a holy environment in the home. The husband sees the change in his wife and is drawn to conversion himself.

A child now has the example of his (or her) parents, to offset the pull of the world. And in the holy environment of that home, it will be much easier for the child to hear the call of God.

The holiness radiates further. Family members find God leading them to become involved in church activities, at school, in the workplace. They meet with others who are being similarly led to live for God, and their combined glow might light the corner of a dark city.

That glow joins with other pockets of light coming to life in the city... in other cities... across the land....

But—it begins with one heart, filled with prayer, creating a holy environment.

# 15

# Living the Messages

In the beginning was the Word, and the Word was God. The Word created the world. It came to Abraham and all his descendents. The Word became flesh, and found its final fulfillment for all mankind in the person of Jesus Christ. In the form of the Gospel, the Word was carried to all the known world by the Apostles. And like God's love, it continually wants to come to man.

At this time in Medjugorje, as a spark igniting a great fire, again the Word comes through a humble and obedient servant, the Blessed Virgin Mary. Her messages to the visionaries—and to the rest of us— are not new. They are as old as the Church itself, and they are simple, easy to understand. She is calling us to pray. To fast. To reconcile. To do penance. To convert.

We have talked about prayer. She has called for each of us to pray for (at least) three hours a day.

For those unused to prayer, that might seem long. For some, even three minutes of unbroken communion with God can be difficult. Do not be discouraged. Those who have been praying all their lives sometimes have difficulty praying through the rosary without their minds behaving like unruly children in church.

Like anything new, prayer takes practice. If you persevere, gradually you will become comfortable in the presence of God. (In time, you will prefer to be there.) If that is forbidding now, begin as Mary has urged, with the rosary.

The first time you dwell on the joyful, sorrowful, and glorious mysteries, you will see that this ancient prayer, while directed to the Mother of God, is actually directing your attention to the life, death, and resurrection of her Son. Even here, she is deferring to Jesus, as she always has.

Her first instruction, given at the wedding feast of Cana in Galilee at the commencement of His earthly ministry, is the same as she gives us now: *Do as He tells you.*

As you become used to prayer, you will become used to the presence of her Son—and His Father.

In the beginning, you may find it easier to create a holy environment in your heart when you yourself are in a holy environment, as in a church. Eventually you will be able to create that environment anywhere. Ultimately it will be there always; you will walk with God, for your life will have become a prayer.

But for now, take it one decade, one Our Father, at a time. There will be much grace on you; all heaven wants you to succeed. You will need the grace, for the evil one and his agents will be trying their hardest to distract and discourage you. An invasion is most easily beaten in the beginning, before it can become established. And that is what is happening in you, as you take prayer seriously: an invasion of holy light. Once that light has established a foothold, it is much harder for the darkness to roll over it.

To help get that foothold on solid ground, you may want to set aside a time each day to pray and listen inwardly—to commune with God. Ask Him when and how long. And then be faithful to it. In the beginning, it may be only a few minutes. But it will grow.

Above all, do not listen when the enemy tells you that you have more important things to do or to think about. Nothing is more important than prayer! And nothing can replace it. With practice, you will simply filter out such harassing thoughts. And you will also learn to ignore negative feelings. At first, it may seem like you are going upstream against them, but persevere. And remember: prayer is like a precision bomb; it will hit the center of your greatest temptation. The main thing is to do it faithfully, for prayer is the hardest habit to form—and the easiest to break.

Like prayer, fasting will be a new thing to the newly converted. It sounds more difficult than it is. And there will be much grace available, because it is a necessary part of the holy life that Jesus calls His disciples to: *If anyone will come after me, let him deny himself, take up his cross, and follow me.*

What manner of fast? Pray and see if whatever was once traditional in your family, your community, your church or your country, needs to be brought back into practice. In Medjugorje, where mothers fast for their children, the tradition is on bread and water, but in

Africa, where there is no bread, it will take some other form. God will show you what is right for you. And remember, while fasting is easier with family and communal support, it can be done alone; Our Lady will support you.

Even with grace, when it comes to self-denial there will be a battle. Perhaps a war. For if we have always indulged the appetites of our flesh, then that flesh will not want us to stop now. At the mere suggestion of it being denied anything, it will throw a tantrum. But if we are to be truly free to follow Christ, then the bondage of its lust must be broken. When lust is mentioned, one usually thinks of the sexual desire, but lust refers to *any* uncontrollable craving. Food, alcohol, tobacco, gossip, even marathon television-watching—all of these things constitute lust of the flesh. You will not have freedom from its tyranny, unless you go to war.

Throughout history, no revolution for freedom's sake has ever succeeded peacefully. The old guard will not let go without a fight. So you must be prepared to go to war within your self.

Either your flesh will have the last word, or your spirit, responding to the Spirit of God, will. And your soul, which will align the force of your will with one side or the other, will decide the outcome.

The enemy's attack will be swift and sure: This is too difficult. Start tomorrow; she's gone to such trouble to prepare your favorite meal. If you don't eat, you won't have the strength to do God's work.

Do not listen. Pray. Ask God to help you. He will. There will be grace sufficient to say no. And if the temptation appears overwhelming, He will provide an escape. You will see; He always does. He will not allow Satan to tempt you beyond your capacity to resist.

Fasting, like prayer, becomes easier with practice. You are building spiritual muscle, and the more you use a muscle, the stronger it becomes. But beware the temptation to spiritual pride. As the Word of God says, no one should be aware, by your face or actions, that you are fasting. If you are doing this for God, then let it be between Him and you.

Do not think that you will need to wage only one war against the flesh. Do you think the enemy is going to give up that easily? He may appear to surrender, but his attacks and temptations will only become more subtle. In other areas of your spiritual life, you already know this: how many inner battles have you had to fight—to sacrifice, to do penance, to forgive a brother who hates you? How many wars have you had to wage against inner selfish attitudes and inclinations? Freedom from self is never bought without a struggle. But those who are willing to sacrifice and fight the good fight courageously, will win.

As you gain practice, you will become a spiritual warrior. Fasting twice a week will not trouble you. And you will be surprised at the ways in which your relationship with God intensifies. You will begin to see things as He sees them. His priorities will become your priorities, and what once seemed so important will now seem unimportant. He will show you areas in your life, where He would have you change—and you will want them to change, also.

As for the fasting, which the enemy and your flesh once tried to convince you was impossible, it will seem a light thing. And eventually, it will become second nature to you, like inward prayer. You will eat sparingly and do *all* things in moderation. In so doing, you will honor God.

Reconciliation—for some, this is harder than prayer or fasting. First, one must become reconciled with God. If you knew Him once and turned away from Him, turn back to him now. It is not too late. If you ask Him, He will forgive you and cleanse your sin and enfold you in His love. But you must ask.

The enemy, of course, will assure you that it is too late. You have been away too long, sunk too low, backslidden too far! God has no use for the likes of you! You deserve hell, and you know it.

Do not listen! Pray! Jesus gave Himself on the Cross for sinners no worse than you. But you must open the lines of communication. Ask, and you shall receive; knock, and it shall be opened unto you....

If you do not know God, the procedure is much the same. But in saying your first prayers, you may have to overcome the logic of your intellect. The enemy will tell you that your imagination is working overtime. Do not listen. Pray. God speaks to us through our hearts, not our heads. Tell Him what He already knows: that there is much in your life you are sorry for, much that you need to be forgiven for. Then ask that forgiveness, and accept it. And with it, the cleansing of Jesus' blood. *Though your sins are like scarlet, they shall be white as snow.* And from that moment onward, let Him be the Master of your life.

Reconciliation with God is perhaps the most difficult for those who have recently lost a loved one. Or been the victim of outrageous fortune. Or had desperate prayer go seemingly unanswered. It is possible to hate God, even when we are certain that such a thing is impossible. Do you blame Him for what happened? Or didn't happen? Do you harbor any negative thoughts whatever towards God? You can be sure that the enemy will confirm them and offer you many more.

If this be the case, the first step of reconciliation is to tell God how you have felt about Him. Then, forgive Him. He works in mysterious ways—that are not our ways. You can trust that He does love you. Far better than an earthly father can love a son or daughter. Sometimes that father must cross a small child's will—and what child has not at some point thought that he hated his father? Even when he also knew that he loved him, and was loved?

When you are ready, God has provided the perfect healing sacraments for reconciliation: Confession and the Eucharist.

Once you are reconciled with God, you must also become reconciled with man. That means forgiving—and that can be difficult indeed. When one has committed an unforgivable sin against you, when one deserves not forgiveness but vengeance—when one deserves hell—then dying can almost seem easier (and preferable).

But—we are called to forgive. Not one time, nor seven, but if necessary, seventy times seven. The act of forgiving is the work of God, and when we forgive, we do His work. It cannot be done without Him. The Lord Himself knows how hard it is. He forgave Judas and those who nailed Him to the Cross. He will provide the necessary grace for us to forgive—anyone, anything. And He calls on us to forgive quickly, before any more calcium drips from the ceiling of our cave to make the stalagmite of unforgiveness even broader.

We are to forgive little slights before they become bigger, minor offenses before they become estrangements. And we are to reconcile estrangements before the gap of separation widens to a chasm. So—when you say "Good morning" to one to whom you would rather not speak, add a smile. And ask God to help you mean it.

What is penance? Repenting in deed, as well as in thought and word. To repent means to turn around and go the other way. To do penance is to do acts of thoughtfulness, where once you might have acted thoughtlessly. Were you selfish? Lazy? Vindictive? Turn and do the opposite. Very simple. Very difficult. Very rewarding. Do you want to be a different person than you were? Acts of penance will help you to change—perhaps faster than anything else.

What, exactly, should I do? God will show you. Ask Him. Have you been close with your money? He may inspire you to acts of generosity greater than you have ever dreamed of! And He will be precise, showing you where, and when, and how. All you have to do is ask—and be open to hear the still, small voice of His Spirit.

Sharing, being unselfish with your time and your self, as well as with your money—giving all you (think you) can and then a little more—has always been part of conversion. Read the stories of the heroes of the faith, and you will see how their conversion and giving go together. When you give freely—and so quickly that the left hand does not realize what the right is doing—then you open areas in your heart to God, which are opened in no other way. Without them, it is like a symphony in which certain notes are missing; it would never sound right.

Which brings us to the underlying theme of the messages: conversion. Evangelicals consider the moment of conversion to be when one acknowledges that he is a sinner, asks God's forgiveness, and accepts him as Lord and Master. In Hercegovina, that is only the beginning: conversion is an ongoing, life-long process, as bit by bit with our cooperation, God conforms us ever more to the image of His Son.

Conversion, then, means staying in touch with the reality of what is going on in us and around us, and dealing with that reality in obedience to God, in faithfulness and in love. We find ourselves constantly asking: "If Jesus were here, what would He do?" Or: "If I am to be holy and to live according to the call and commandments of God, what do I need to do now?"

To be holy does not mean to be strange; a fanatic or a freak. It means to be a very normal, healthy, balanced person. Forget what the world or the devil might tell you: it is normal to live a holy life, for that is the life that God created you to live. Holiness means wholeness.

A holy person is unimposing. He does not stand out or draw attention to himself. Even when challenged or required in difficult times to respond courageously, it is only normal to his call.

A holy person is often silent. That is another fast I would suggest: fasting from unnecessary words. Too many people do not appreciate silence. They do not know how to use it constructively. Uncomfortable in it, especially in the company of others, they throw words around carelessly. In a case of one opinion against another, they must emerge victorious. If they have done something commendable, they are not content to let God be the only one who knows.

In silence they could accomplish wonderful things for their families! They could express a willingness to serve, and let their loving presence speak for them. Their ego would be denied its lust for recognition and approval, but Jesus in them would be seen. And He would be glorified.

The wiser and more humble the pilgrim, the greater his appreciation for the power of words. And the fewer he uses. Words are more powerful than any tool—or weapon—you can hold in your hand. With words, God created the world. With words you can create—or destroy—the world of your family, the environment in which your children will grow. Use them with great care—and with love.

Just as the war with the world, the flesh, and the devil never ends, neither does the process of—or the need for—conversion. A few years ago, a Catholic priest from America was shocked when the visionary Maria privately asked him to pray for her conversion. Few people here have a more intimate relationship with the Holy Family than she does, yet she coveted this priest's prayers. It was precisely her willingness to be searched by God's light which had revealed to her how much in her soul still needed to be sanctified.

And she knew that she could not do it alone. She needed the help and the prayers of others. And so do you and I. To live the messages of Medjugorje, we need the companionship and support of others who are on the same path. If you do not know any, ask God to help. He will put you in touch with them.

Soon, you will find yourself in the company of a good band of life's pilgrims. It will be easier, then, to live the message of Our Lady, which is the message of the Gospel.

You will be more than just living it; you will *be* the message.

# 16

# Pray for Medjugorje

God is our Creator. He knows the way we function and exist, and He would like to create us once again. So in Medjugorje, man is being created anew. Through prayer, fasting, reconciliation, penance, peace—and conversion—the work which Jesus Christ began on earth is being continued. The work of the Church is being brought to perfection.

Medjugorje is playing a part in this work. Every pilgrim who comes here, leaves different than when he or she came. They may not accept the apparitions; they may even find much to criticize. But they cannot deny the power of the impact that Medjugorje is having on those around them.

When they go home, they may speak against it. Or, they may speak too soon *for* it—before the messages have begun to become a reality in their lives. But they will not be indifferent to it. And when they look back on their pilgrimage, they will see their journey to Medjugorje as a major event in their lives.

On the cover of a recent issue of *Life*, one of the major magazines in America, is the picture of the statue of Our Lady which stands in the plaza before St James Church. The cover story is as fair as one could expect from an objective journalist writing for a secular publication. (I suspect that the new wine is continuing to ferment.)

I smile to recall that young priest in New York, so desperate to inform editors and producers of what was occurring in the mountains of his native Hercegovina. God has His timetable—and it would seem that Medjugorje's time is now. Enough time has elapsed, enough lives have been changed. Enough miracles have happened—not only the physical healings, but the more amazing transformations of the heart. People leave here free. They are free from their old natures, free from the bondage of self. They go home to live the messages that Our Lady has been giving—and if they persevere, they themselves become the message of Medjugorje.

It would seem that Mary's time is also now. Satan is not to have the close of this century to himself.

In the Garden of Eden, God said that He would put enmity between the woman and the serpent—and so He has.

She is everywhere, warning people of his wiles, neutralizing his poison with the antidote of perfect love. How can she be in so many places at once, and also interceding for us to the Father? I don't have to know. I am content to leave it a holy mystery. But I am very grateful for it. I imagine that in this special mission, this final assignment, she is not constrained by time or place, as we are. Bethlehem, Guadeloupe, Lourdes, Fatima, Medjugorje, and the others—they are all one single embrace of a mother for her children, for the whole Church.

Meanwhile, she continues to return to the mountain village in Hercegovina every day at the same time. Her messages have grown shorter—but no less urgent. With good reason: the world has become a precarious place to live. The streets of many large cities, east and west, have become almost battle zones, and many people are living on the sharp edge of disaster.

But she has help now. She repeatedly asked for our help—and she is receiving it. All over the world people are praying with her for peace, for lost souls to be reunited with their Maker. The sand in the hourglass may be almost running out, but the strength of those prayers is growing, as each day more are added to the number of the faithful.

It is my hope—and prayer—that what is happening here might in some way be responsible for adding one vocation—one extra priest, one extra sister— to every diocese in the world. I would also pray that those already in vocations would have their spiritual lives enriched, and the quality of their life improved, by Medjugorje. And I would pray that in the family, mothers and fathers would be touched—and inspired to a new appreciation of the divine calling of parenthood.

I would pray for God to give the gift of wisdom to those who go away from here on fire to tell the world about Medjugorje. Anyone who has met God here—who has reached out and touched Him with their mind—has experienced a miracle. It is natural to want to share something so extraordinary, especially with those one loves. It takes great wisdom to realize that someone else simply cannot fully appreciate such a thing second-hand. Yet if one allows the inner miracle to continue—to the point where it begins to change the life of the one to whom it has happened— then others will be moved to reach out themselves....

I would pray that each pilgrim who comes here would be content with the call of God he receives. Some will have received it a long time ago and will have it renewed here. Others will receive it here—and for a few it may be spectacular. There is no question that God places a universal, prophetic calling on every individual. I have seen Him call simple people here on pilgrimage—and then anoint them powerfully and send them forth to do wonderful, miraculous things for the Church and for the world. Often this happens to housewives with no special training—they are used to change the lives of hundreds of people. And no one is too little to be used for great things.

But sadly I have also seen people who wanted so badly to do such things that they have mistaken their own desire for the call of God. And so I would pray for wisdom—and humility—for *all* who come here. If you have been chosen to be a special, high-profile messenger, you will know it. If you have not been so chosen, then be content with the call which every one of us has received: to live the messages. If you will do that, your life will one day be used by God to affect other lives—and you may never even be aware of it. Many are called, but few are chosen.... And those chosen are usually the last to seek it; they think God has made a mistake. "Surely not me, God! Don't you have someone else?" God has a sense of humor; He often chooses the foolish things of this world to confound the wise.

So—that is how I am praying for Medjugorje.

If you would like to pray for Medjugorje, there are a few areas which would benefit from your prayers. The main area of concern would be the hearts of the people of Medjugorje. The pull and temptations of the world are much stronger now. The Blessed Mother has called them to serve the pilgrims and open their hearts to them, without thought of compensation. But the pilgrims are often so grateful for what is happening to them that they thrust extra money upon their hosts, on passersby, on everybody. They mean well— God has quickened their hearts to be generous, some of them for the first time in their lives. But now suddenly all of this money comes, when for centuries there had been so little....

For some the temptation has proven to be more than they have been able to withstand. They build additions onto their houses, so that they can take in more pilgrims. They join others in building hotels; they buy cars they would never have dreamed of owning before.

These are not bad things in themselves. But some of the local people are losing sight of what the Blessed Mother has called them to, the mission she has given their whole parish. They look about them and see souvenir hawkers and cab-drivers who have come from as far away as Mostar, to get some of the pilgrims' money, and they think, well, why not my family? Do not my children deserve all that I can give them? And ever so subtly, getting becomes more important than giving. The grace and inspiration to give is present, but so is the temptation to greed.

Then, too, among so many dedicated friends coming to help carry on the work of God here, invariably some come with their own agenda. Some guides of pilgrims come to lead, but they mislead. Others caught in sin come seeking to be delivered—but they draw others into their sin. Pilgrims in confusion wind up confusing others. New Age gurus attempt to turn Medjugorje into a New Age center, devoid of the Sacraments and the centrality of Christ.

What, then, is one to do? One cannot stand guard like some Don Quixote, trying to protect and control everything. The Holy Spirit, through the believers and in a special way, the priests, creates a holy environment, one in which the evil one is not comfortable and departs. In this way the Living Water in the spring that is Medjugorje, is kept pure.

Here is where the prayers of the friends of Medjugorje give a tremendous help. Please pray for the protection of the hearts and souls of the local people. Pray for the purity of the motives of those who come to help. Pray for the conversion of all "seekers" who do not have God as the focus of their pilgrimage.

Please pray for the visionaries, and pray for the people of Medjugorje, for them to stay faithful to their commitment, for them to stay holy, and to continue to pass on the fruit of their ongoing conversion to their families, to their church, and to their countries. And pray that for all the friends of Medjugorje. The greatest threat to this place is weakness and failures in the hearts of those who love what God is doing here.

Finally, please pray for, the spirit of unity to prevail—here, and throughout the world. When Christ returns, all who love Him and are called by His name will be gathered into one Church anyway, but in the meantime, let our love for God bind us together as brothers and sisters, regardless of whether we are from the East or the West, Protestant, Orthodox or Roman Catholic. The spirit of disunity, with its separation and hatred and mistrust, has prevailed for too long. If we will return to the Gospel, and accept that Jesus Christ is who He said He was, then as we kneel at the foot of His Cross, we will be truly one.

What shall I say now, as we come to the end? If you are coming to Medjugorje, be happy, for your pilgrimage will be a living, unfolding prayer. But remember: the purpose of this place is not for you to fall in love with it. Medjugorje does not want to control you or possess you for itself in any way. But God does want you for Himself.

Fall in love with God!

# 17

# Sunset

The newest of our mission churches in Konjic stands on the side of a mountain, several hundred meters above the Bijela River. The bell tower still lacks a bell, but in less than four years it has become a stronghold of faith and prayer. One day, its bell will pray the prayer of Angelus in the morning, at noontime, and in the evening over the entire valley.

In back of the church is a small rocky promontory that juts out over the river. It is a solitary place, with barely enough room for one person to sit. Sometimes I come here to watch the sun go down.

It is always peaceful here. And it takes only a few minutes for the surrounding mountains to bring God's order back into your life. They are higher and more severe than other mountains in Hercegovina—to the south, the peak called Prenj still has snow in its crevices, and it is the middle of July.

But for all their height, they are not as barren as the mountains at home. Cula and her gang of lambs would grow fat, grazing on the grassy foothill across the river.

The sound of the water rushing over the little dam below is so soothing; in half an hour it could blunt the barbs of the most thorny problem—and often has.

In the final hour of daylight, the valley is bathed in soft, golden hues. The dwellings are nestled close to the ground, like small birds sheltering for the night. Under their red-tiled roofs, evening meals are being prepared. A rooster crows, a dog barks, some children are playing.

Some of these families are Moslem, some are Orthodox, some are Catholic. But they live together in peace. The mountains have taught them to be good neighbors.

I wish that were so for the rest of my country. At this moment, tanks are poised at the borders of Hercegovina, ready to enter at the slightest excuse.

The history of this land has been written in blood. World War I began here, and while for the rest of Europe the threat of World War III is now a receding bad dream, here it is an ongoing nightmare. Other East Bloc countries, recognizing Communism as morally and ideologically bankrupt, have been able to shed it with little or no loss of life. In free elections, for some the first in thirty-five years, they have chosen to go the way of democracy. So have the Slovenians and Croatians.

But here the old guard is loathe to let go. They would prefer to keep the people shackled to a corpse. And so, in recent days the evening news has been filled with tragic scenes of young freedom fighters to the north who have been killed or wounded—amateur soldiers attempting to battle jets and heavy armor with rifles.

Yesterday, Saturday, a caravan of young people was driving from Citluk to Medjugorje—perhaps twenty cars in all, waving gaily as they passed. They might have been coming from a wedding celebration, but from the window of the lead car flew a great flag with three broad stripes of red, white and blue with a red-and-white checkered shield in the center. This was the flag of Croatia, and on this bright, sunny afternoon these young men and women were laughing and happy—in love with the idea of independence. But if there was civil war, no one would be laughing for a long time.

For the moment, the generals give the appearance of accepting civilian authority. But there is little doubt that at the least provocation, they will move with great force to crush the movement which threatens their hold on power. Then these mountains will once again be wreathed in artillery smoke and will echo with the sounds of war. And in the Provincial Office in Mostar, the ancient leather-bound ledger will receive fresh names of friars and priests who will not compromise.

It does not have to be. If those who love Medjugorje will again heed the appeal of the Blessed Mother and pray for peace, they can make the difference. She has said that prayer can stop wars. Millions of pilgrims have believed her and have prayed with the heart for peace. The answers to those prayers have been stunning.

Now, here, there is a greater need for such prayers than ever before. Your prayers can save Medjugorje—and Hercegovina, and all this tortured land. Will you pray?

The mountains across the river are dark, misty outlines now, and twilight rises quickly from the valley below. Only the tops of the mountains to the east are still in daylight, and they are burnished red-gold by the last rays of the setting sun.

By my left foot is a lone thistle, its lavender flower in stark contrast against the gathering darkness across the valley. There is a similar thistle marking a similar secluded spot on Podbrdo, not far from where Our Lady first appeared. More than once I have watched the sun set over Medjugorje from there. In each place a thistle—it is as if God were saying that such places, so ideal for reflection, do not occur by accident.

Now the sky is darkening to match the silhouettes of the mountains. The mountains—I would gladly remain here among them forever, like a small bird nestled in the hollow of God's hand. But the bell of our church in Konjic will soon be calling, and I must go.